YOSEMITE TAHOE

Weekend Adventure getaways

YOSEMITE TAHOE

Weekend Adventure getaways

RICHARD HARRIS

PHOTOGRAPHY BY LEE FOSTER

Ulysses Press

Published by:
Ulysses Press
P.O. Box 3440
Berkeley, CA 94703
www.ulyssespress.com

ISBN 1-56975-384-9
ISSN 1545-5629

Printed in Canada by Transcontinental Printing
10 9 8 7 6 5 4 3 2 1

Front cover photography: arttoday.com
Back cover photography: Lee Foster
Design: Sarah Levin, Leslie Henriques
Editorial and production: Claire Chun, Lily Chou, Steven Schwartz
Maps: Pease Press
Index: Sayre Van Young

Distributed in the United States by Publishers Group West
and in Canada by Raincoast Books

write to us

If in your travels you discover a spot that captures the spirit of Yosemite and Lake Tahoe, or if you live in the region and have a favorite place to share, or if you just feel like expressing your views, write to us and we'll pass your note along to the author.

We can't guarantee that the author will add your personal find to the next edition, but if the writer does use the suggestion, we'll acknowledge you in the credits and send you a free copy of the new edition.

ULYSSES PRESS
P.O. Box 3440
Berkeley, CA 94703
E-mail: readermail@ulyssespress.com

table of contents

MAPS

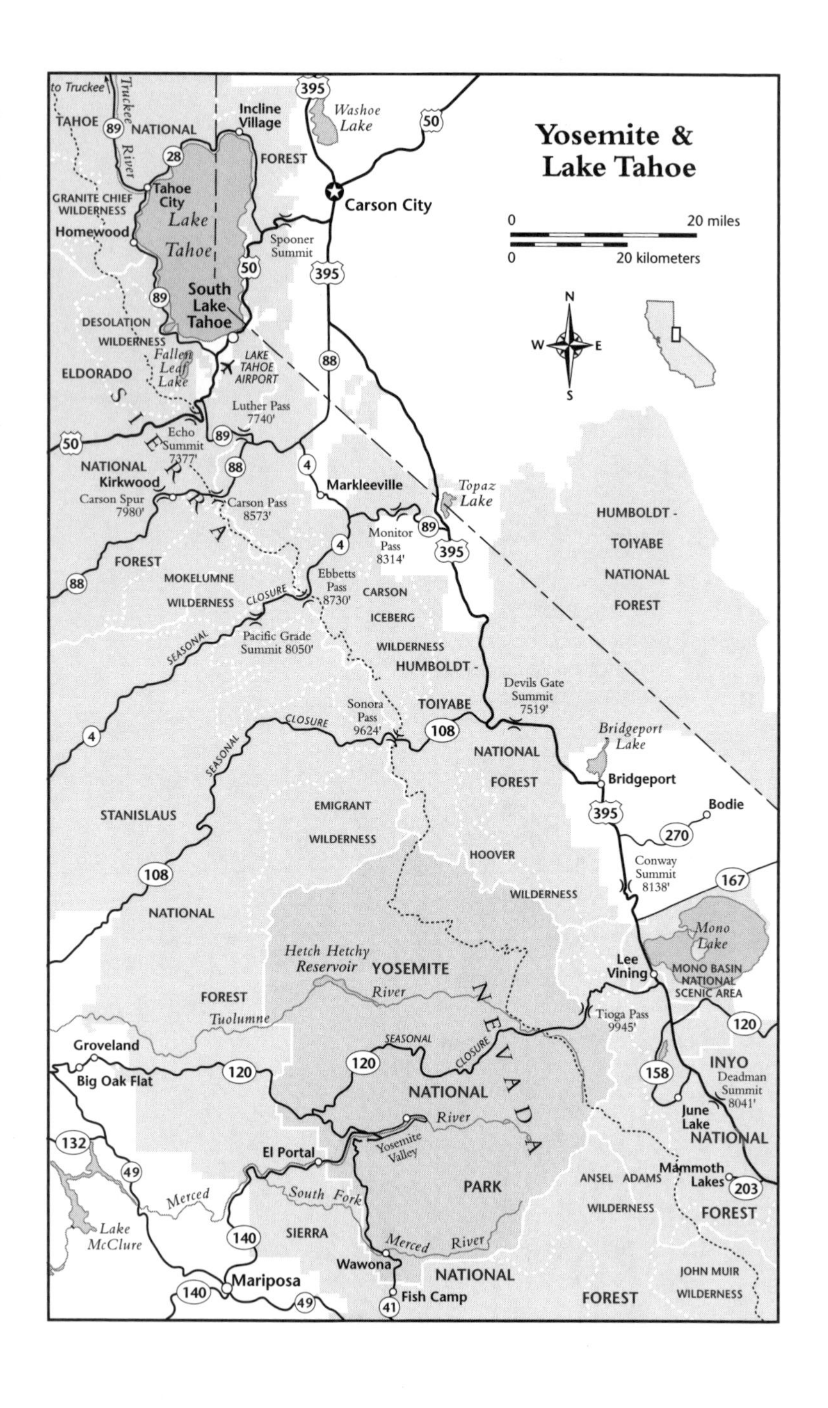

Yosemite & Lake Tahoe
0
20 miles
0
20 kilometers
N
S
E
W
to Truckee
Truckee River
TAHOE NATIONAL FOREST
Incline Village
Washoe Lake
Tahoe City
GRANITE CHIEF WILDERNESS
Homewood
Lake Tahoe
Carson City
Spooner Summit
South Lake Tahoe
DESOLATION WILDERNESS
Fallen Leaf Lake
LAKE TAHOE AIRPORT
ELDORADO NATIONAL FOREST
Luther Pass 7740'
Echo Summit 7377'
Kirkwood
Carson Spur 7980'
Carson Pass 8573'
Markleeville
Topaz Lake
Monitor Pass 8314'
Ebbetts Pass 8730'
MOKELUMNE WILDERNESS
CARSON ICEBERG WILDERNESS
SEASONAL CLOSURE
Pacific Grade Summit 8050'
HUMBOLDT - TOIYABE NATIONAL FOREST
Devils Gate Summit 7519'
Sonora Pass 9624'
Bridgeport Lake
Bridgeport
Bodie
STANISLAUS NATIONAL FOREST
EMIGRANT WILDERNESS
HOOVER WILDERNESS
Conway Summit 8138'
Mono Lake
Lee Vining
MONO BASIN NATIONAL SCENIC AREA
Hetch Hetchy Reservoir
YOSEMITE NATIONAL PARK
Tuolumne River
Tioga Pass 9945'
SIERRA NEVADA
Groveland
Big Oak Flat
INYO NATIONAL FOREST
Deadman Summit 8041'
June Lake
Yosemite Valley
Merced River
El Portal
South Fork
Mammoth Lakes
ANSEL ADAMS WILDERNESS
Lake McClure
SIERRA NATIONAL FOREST
Wawona
Mariposa
Fish Camp
JOHN MUIR WILDERNESS
395
50
89
28
88
4
108
270
167
120
158
132
49
140
41
203

1

Yosemite & Lake Tahoe

The spirit of California's High Sierra permeates Yosemite National Park and Lake Tahoe, two world-class mountain destinations that are as similar as siblings and, at the same time, as different. Robed in evergreen forests, speckled with small alpine lakes, covered with snowdrifts up to 40 feet deep in winter and agleam with slender, glacier-packed crevices even in midsummer, each provides a haven for visitors in the heart of a vast wilderness, a respite that seems far removed in time as well as space from the hurried life-styles of wherever in the world you happen to come from. Each of them was once so well hidden that American Indian people lived there in safety from their enemies.

Yet Yosemite and Lake Tahoe have evolved along different paths. Under the stewardship of state and

federal park administrators since the mid-19th century, Yosemite has clung to its pristine character by means of ever more sophisticated crowd-control measures; yet it has also opened the best of the deep wilderness to countless thousands of people who might otherwise never experience it. Lake Tahoe, on the other hand, is what Yosemite might have become if its old-time tourist development had continued—a free-enterprise zone half-filled with golf courses, gaming casinos, ski resorts and boat cruises. You can mountain-bike down one of the most dramatic rides in the Sierra, soar in a hot-air balloon, catch and release a 30-pound Mackinaw lake trout and still be back in time for dinner in your choice of dozens of exceptional restaurants, casual or elegant.

Today, instead of being unified as Yosemite is, about half the shoreline of Lake Tahoe is protected as one part of three national forests or one of several California and Nevada state parks. The result has been a greater emphasis on conservation at Yosemite and on

Opposite: El Capitan, Yosemite.

recreation at Lake Tahoe. In Yosemite, a decision was made in the 1970s not to stock the streams and lakes with trout, yet visitors were allowed to fish; as a result, your chances of actually catching a fish in Yosemite today are slim to none. In the lakes of the mountain wilderness surrounding Lake Tahoe, hundreds of thousands of fingerling trout are dumped from airplanes each year to replace the mature ones that are caught by all the anglers who hike in for miles to fish there.

Without dwelling too long on which approach would be more likely to make Yosemite explorer, naturalist and Sierra Club founder John Muir roll over in his grave, I can say with enthusiasm that both Yosemite and Lake Tahoe, in their different unique styles, offer the widest imaginable range of adventures amid natural settings guaranteed to take your breath away. Personally, my passion is for wilderness hiking. I first experienced the High Sierra as a child on family camping trips. In the decades since, I've returned many times and trekked to such memorable places as Yosemite's dramatic Grand Canyon of the Tuolumne River and the idyllic Lake Aloha near Lake Tahoe. Somewhere along those trails, it dawned on me that I'll never exhaust the Sierra's myriad hiking possibilities. All I can do is share the ones I know about. Other visitors I meet, whose sporting tastes run the gamut from rock climbing to kayaking, from telemarking to flyfishing and from snowshoeing to golf, say much the same thing. Whatever enlivens your mind, body and spirit, chances are you'll find it in the High Sierra in such amazing abundance that deciding where to go next may be the biggest challenge of all.

geography

The High Sierra lies roughly 150 miles east of San Francisco and extends 430 miles from Plumas County in the north to Sequoia National Park's Mount Whitney in the south, spanning half the length of California. The mountains are officially named the Sierra Nevada, Spanish for "Snowy Range," though it remained an unexplored presence on the distant horizon throughout the Spanish Colonial era.

In common parlance, many people subdivide the Gold Country, the western foothills of the Sierra Nevada, which were thoroughly explored and occupied by prospectors, miners and boomtown entrepreneurs in the great Gold Rush of 1849, from the High Sierra, the often snowbound realm which only grudgingly disclosed its secrets to a handful of mountain men back in those days and still remains mostly unsettled today. Only six highways cross from one side of the High Sierra to the other, and three of them are closed in the winter. One county in the High Sierra is larger than the San Francisco Bay Area and has a population of only 1200.

The Sierra Nevada slopes gently upward from west to east. Moisture that rolls in from the Pacific eases up the mountain slopes, cooling as it rises and condensing into heavy rains and snowfalls. By the time a weather front reaches the far side, the High Sierra has sucked it dry, thus the valleys beyond receive so little precipitation that they form a vast desert in the "rain shadow" of the Sierra. The sagebrush and creosote bush wastelands and rippling sand dunes of areas such as Death Valley are part of the same phenomenon as the lush forests of the high country.

flora

The giant sequoias found in about 75 scattered groves in the Sierra Nevada, including three in Yosemite, are so big and old that it's easy to think of everything else as just trees. Yet in both Yosemite and the Lake Tahoe area, lace up your hiking boots and it's easy to experience the amazing diversity of ancient, pristine forest.

OPPOSITE: Grizzly Giant in Mariposa Grove Big Trees.

You may or may not be interested in learning how to tell a lodgepole pine from a sugar pine or a white fir from a Douglas fir. In fact, you may or may not be interested in distinguishing an aspen from an oak. What will help you enjoy the wilderness more is to notice the differences between tree species, especially conifers like pines, fir and spruces. Everywhere you look, the trees that make up a forest change. Different species grow at different elevations. Different ones grow in shady places than sunny ones. Different ones grow beside streams than on ridgelines. Trees speak eloquently about the land that surrounds you as you travel in the mountains. Take time to look at the exhibits in the visitors centers at Yosemite and Lake Tahoe and learn a little more about the world we live in.

Size isn't everything. When spring comes to the high country (sometime in June), one of the most amazing sights in the Sierra is the profusion of wildflowers that bursts forth in the heady mixture of snowmelt and high-altitude sunlight. Most of the flowers are tiny—you could make them into doll-size bouquets if picking them were not against the law—and they cover the high meadows in such abundance that they shimmer like the dots in a pointillist painting. Visitors exhibits or a wildflower field guide can help you name them; the problem is that they appear, spread their beauty to the wind and vanish so quickly that if you come back the next weekend, a riot of lupines and paintbrushes may have replaced the phloxes and brilliant scarlet gilia you saw there before.

Even the grass leads an interesting life in the High Sierra. Unlike the bluegrass and other wet climate grasses that we're used to seeing in suburban lawns, the natural grasses of the Sierra Nevada change colors with the weather, not the season of the year. In dry spells, mountain grasses turn as golden as hay. But after a thunderstorm, when the roots find moisture, chlorophyll surges through the blades of grass and, like a chameleon, a whole meadow can turn brilliant green in the course of an afternoon. This is what the mountains can teach us if we pay attention: They are alive.

fauna

Many visitors to Yosemite and Lake Tahoe wonder why they don't see more animals. Oh, sure, squirrels and maybe at high altitudes an occasional yellow-bellied marmot, but I'm talking about *real* animals. Coyotes. Mountain sheep. Bears.

The fact is, these and many other large animals live in the High Sierra. An estimated 700 black bears live within the boundaries of Yosemite National Park alone. But since more than 95 percent of Yosemite is roadless wilderness, much of it densely wooded and some of it completely inaccessible to humans, stumbling upon a bear or mountain lion by surprise is relatively unlikely.

A decade ago in Yosemite, there were many more encounters between humans and black bears than there are today. Many bears had learned that humans were a great food source—not that any black bear has ever been known to eat a human, but that ice chests, garbage cans and just about anyplace else where humans put uneaten food were easy pickings for a bear trying to fatten up for the winter's hibernation.

Because of the risks that bear encounters held for bears and humans alike, the National Park Service adopted regulations requiring visitors to store their food in bearproof boxes and little by little Yosemite's bears learned that filching properly protected human food was more trouble than it was worth. Along with these regulations, the park service started capturing overly persistent "problem" bears and moving them by helicopter to more remote parts of the wilderness. Today, encounters between humans and bears have declined, though such incidents still occur at a rate of more than two a day during the summer.

Encounters between humans and mountain lions, however, are sharply on the increase. No one knows why for sure. Mountain lions don't eat either human food or humans (except very small ones), though one of them may sometimes snatch a small dog or cat if the opportunity arises. Park service and forest service people believe the problem comes down to the fact that more and more hikers are invading their domain, and since they've been protected as an endangered species, mountain lions may have become less timid about humans. Under these circumstances, they're bound to cross paths once in a while.

It may help to remember the old adage, "They're more afraid of you than you are of them." Or it may not. The important thing to keep in mind is that the Sierra is home to myriad wild animals, and we're just visiting. Whether it's the thrill of watching through binoculars as male bighorn sheep clash on a distant granite ridge, or of glimpsing a mountain lion as it dashes past your headlights, or of staring in amazement as your golf ball barely misses a deer grazing on the 17th fairway, every wild animal encounter is an experience to remember.

If encounters with large mammals are uncommon, birds are almost a constant presence in the Sierra. Along creeks and rivers you may see sparrows, blackbirds, starlings and kingfishers. Lake shallows and wetlands invite herons and migrating waterfowl. Conifer forests teem with Stellar's jays and Gray's jays, among others. High mountain crags are patrolled by ravens, vultures and occasional eagles, and in the spring parts of Yosemite are restricted to avoid disturbing the nests of peregrine falcons. Wherever you go, you're bound to encounter what serious birders refer to as "LYBs"—little yellow birds—and their gray and brown cousins. Whenever you feel a desire for greater closeness with your natural surroundings, the simplest way is to pay attention to the birds you see and hear around you. American Indians claimed birds were messengers from the spirit world, and if you watch them, it may soon become apparent that they inhabit a universe parallel to our own.

Half Dome.

geology

The largest single mountain range in the United States, the Sierra Nevada is essentially a huge block of the earth's crust, tilted and uplifted as the tectonic plate that lies under the Pacific Ocean collided with the Continental Plate under the United States east of California. In fact, the uplifting continues today—but very slowly, giving our imaginations some sense of the true meaning of geological time.

Although the great granite domes of Yosemite are remnants of a far older mountain range that vanished beneath the sea many millions of years before the present Sierra Nevada began to take shape, California did not assume anything resembling its present form until around 750,000 years ago. Even then, the high country looked more like gently rolling hills and valleys until a series of Ice Ages from around 50,000 to 10,000 years ago sent glaciers flowing down the slopes, carving solid cliffs with abrasive layers of rocks and gravel under unimaginable weights of ice. As they melted, what remained was the Sierra Nevada. Some features of the ice-sculpted terrain are unique—like the Yosemite Valley, sliced so sheer that stream water flowing into it may plunge hundreds of feet without touching the side of the cliff, or the Lake Tahoe Basin, gouged so deep that before the water could flow over the edge and down the Truckee River, its level had to rise high enough to make Lake Tahoe the second-deepest lake in the United States.

Biking in Yosemite.

when to go

Some of us plan our vacations around the four seasons. You'll experience some of California's most dramatic weather in the Sierra Nevada. Yet far from scaring off visitors, the changeable climate broadens the array of outdoor activities into a year-round adventure-seekers' smorgasbord. In Yosemite, though summer is by far the busiest time, discriminating travelers come throughout the off-season to savor the park's solitude and crystalline beauty, bike riding by day and relaxing by a roaring fire in one of the park's lodges after dusk. Lake Tahoe, with its world-class ski slopes, doesn't experience much down-time; the fall and spring "off-seasons" now occupy weeks, not months, on the calendar, and with the success of South Lake Tahoe's new convention center, they may soon dwindle down to an occasional slow weekend.

In summer, when both Yosemite and Lake Tahoe are cluttered with visitors, you can expect warm—even hot—days and sweater-cool nights. Even at that, what you expect isn't always what you get. Although California enjoys a "Mediterranean" weather pattern, meaning that it tends to be dry in the summer months and wet in the winter, it's not unusual for thunderstorm clouds to billow into the sky, pouring rain, spitting lightning and dropping the temperature by 30 degrees in 30 minutes. In Yosemite, major trails carry near-capacity hiking and

Mono Lake.

horseback traffic, while rock climbers dangle overhead and park shuttles enable less athletic visitors to explore all day. Lake Tahoe's trails tend to be less congested with hikers, but only because so many other activities (e.g., mountain biking, sportfishing, golf, waterskiing, hot-air ballooning, casino gaming) vie for visitors' attention.

As fall arrives and the hordes return home, the display of fall colors in the high country is breathtaking, like nothing you see in the milder climes along the California coast. Foremost are the aspen trees, found in groves over a wide belt of elevations both in Yosemite and around Lake Tahoe. Some spots, such as North Canyon above Lake Tahoe—Nevada State Park's Spooner Lake, are so well known for their aspen displays that fall, not summer or ski season, is their busiest time. In the riparian vegetation zone along Yosemite's Merced River, the diversity of trees and bushes paints the landscape with a palette of hues so varied that it may make your soul sing. Perfect daytime temperatures and sunshine prevail, though if you're camping, around 7 p.m. you may start to notice that you can see your breath. Around Lake Tahoe there's an early November lull before the slopes start opening. Many local residents shut down their businesses and go on vacation for the first two or three weeks of November. Room rates around Lake Tahoe drop into the bargain price range until the first snowfall, and visitors find that Lake Tahoe itself looks even more beautiful without thousands of boats congesting its surface; on weekdays, you can practically have the lake to yourself. Although nighttime temperatures may prove a little nippy for overnight camping, fall is a pretty, uncrowded time for day-hiking and mountain biking. Hikers can find solitude on Yosemite's backcountry trails at this time of year, too. Unlike at Tahoe, however, lodging rates don't go down during the off-season; instead, the park service closes its camping cabins when the leaves fall from the trees, and reservations at the remaining lodges are as hard to get as ever.

Winter swaddles Yosemite in a blanket of white silence, closing down the road into the high country as well as the campgrounds. Yet winter in Yosemite also means the opening of folksy little Badger Pass Ski Area, the oldest ski slope in California. Some backcountry trails are also groomed for cross-country skiing. A nonstop parade of holiday events, including lavish Thanksgiving, Christmas and New Year's celebrations as well as a series of culinary fests featuring world-renowned chefs and vintners, take place at the elegant Ahwahnee Hotel. Lake Tahoe is as lively in winter as in summer, with superb alpine skiing and hundreds of miles of cross-country trails. Because its depths capture the sun's warmth in summer, Lake Tahoe's surface never freezes; a few diehard anglers brave potentially blustery weather in hopes of hooking Tahoe's legendary Mackinaw trout, which prefer frigid water and swim much closer to the surface in winter.

Springtime comes late to the High Sierra. One may speculate that when 1930s musical star Nelson Eddy was singing to Jeanette MacDonald about springtime in the Rockies on the shore of an alpine lake near the Tahoe shore (okay, so it wasn't *really* the Rockies, but then, Eddy wasn't really a Canadian mountie either), they were probably standing in slush. But when the snow finally melts away and wildflowers spray across the meadows so suddenly that you almost expect to hear the bangs of skyrockets, you'll know what he was crooning about. You may still need your parka after dark. The snowmelt in the High Sierra reaches its peak between mid-April and mid-June. If breathtaking waterfalls are among your favorite things, that's the time to go.

packing & preparation

At the top of the list of things to take on any Yosemite or Lake Tahoe trip is the sporting equipment you need for your choice among the many recreational opportunities there. This could mean gear as portable as a flyfishing tackle box, a bag of golf clubs or a backpack, tent and sleeping bag. It could involve the challenge of wrestling mountain bikes or a kayak onto your car's roof rack. Or it could require hauling a powerboat or a horse trailer up mountain roads. When it comes to adventure, each of us shapes our own travel style.

Besides sports gear, your car or RV can probably carry more than you will actually need. Many people tend to overpack because anticipation of a vacation trip can manifest itself in thoughts like, "What if we find a roadside stand selling fresh vegetables . . . . We might want the electric wok!" Packing light, a common adventure travel mantra, may keep us from feeling silly when we look at all the extraneous stuff we brought along, but the fact remains, as road trippers we can usually find a spot somewhere, under a seat or in a corner of the trunk, for the wok and anything else we feel compelled to bring. The problem is, after a couple of days on the road and living out of our vehicles in campgrounds or motels, all that carefully packed stuff starts to expand like an air bag, filling the whole car or motorhome with laundry, unfolded maps, mini-shampoo bottles, rolls of film and empty corn chip bags, as well as all the other items we had to rummage through to find the ones we wanted to pull out. At that point we realize that backpack travelers have it right: Pack light!

Cross-country skiing at Badger Pass.

Lake Tahoe.

The key consideration for visiting Yosemite and Lake Tahoe at any time of year is to plan your clothing in layers—the more and thinner, the better. A crisp flannel-shirt fall morning can turn hot enough for a tank top in about two hours, then blow up sweeping rain sprinkles that call for a windbreaker and stocking cap. Natural silk and high-tech skiwear fabrics provide superior insulation and store easily in a daypack. If all the layers are color-coordinated, you can also pass for well-dressed at almost any restaurant in Yosemite or Lake Tahoe.

Even in winter, cross-country skiing and other sustained exercise can heat things up so that you'll want to remove your parka and wear just your T-shirt. When you stop, it will instantly be cold again, so it's best if you can strip down and carry your parka in your pack. Avoid wearing jeans for winter sports. The cotton absorbs snow that melts from your body heat, weighing you down with snowpack, slowly soaking your jeans with ice water and placing you at risk for hypothermia. Wool pants are the time-honored solution. Modern poly-pro or fleece clothing offers more protection and comfort.

visitors centers

The **Yosemite National Park Visitors Center** at Yosemite Village in Yosemite Valley has museum-style exhibits, a bookstore and an information desk where park rangers can help you plan for hikes and other activities. ~ 209-372-0200; www.nps.gov/yose. Yosemite also has several **Wilderness Centers** where you can get a wilderness permit, a bearproof food canister, maps and the answers to all your questions about the trail ahead.

The place to go for ranger advice and maps in the Lake Tahoe area is the U.S. Forest Service's **Taylor Creek Visitors Center**, where besides a bookstore and information desk there are miles of easy nature trails. Open late May through September, weekends only through October. ~ Lake Tahoe Basin Management Unit, 530-573-2674; www.r5.fs.fed.us/ltbmu.

Lake Tahoe also has a profusion of Chambers of Commerce and Convention and Visitors Bureaus, most with their own tourist centers that offer tourist brochures, free information from organizations such as state parks, ski and bike associations and guidance from local volunteers. They include: **Lake Tahoe Visitors Authority** (1156 Ski Run Boulevard, South Lake Tahoe; 530-544-5050, 800-288-2463; www.virtualtahoe.com), **South Lake Tahoe Chamber of Commerce** (3066 Lake Tahoe Boulevard, South Lake Tahoe; 530-541-5255), **North Lake Tahoe Chamber of Commerce** (245 North Lake Boulevard, Tahoe City; 530-581-6900), **Truckee-Donner Chamber of Commerce** (10065 Commercial Row, Truckee; 530-587-2757, 800-548-8388; www.truckee.com), **Incline Village—Crystal Bay Chamber of Commerce** (969 Tahoe Boulevard, Incline Village; 775-4440) and the **Tahoe-Douglas Chamber of Commerce and Visitor Center** (I195 Route 50, Stateline; 775-588-4591; www.tahoechamber.org).

hiking

For a lot of people, hiking is the main reason to visit Yosemite National Park, where hundreds of miles of backcountry trails lead to some of the most spectacular natural landscapes in the High Sierra, such as Muir Gorge and the Grand Canyon of the Tuolumne River, which can only be seen by hiking there.

Some visitors to Lake Tahoe may not even realize the many hiking possibilities. Trailheads are not often conspicuous, and the looming rim around the lake blocks our awareness of the vast mountain expanses that lie just beyond. The Tahoe Rim Trail, the longest trek in the area, follows the highest ridgelines from Lake Tahoe. Some trails, like the one to incomparable Lake Aloha, take hikers into the Desolation Wilderness. Others ascend into the Granite Chief Wilderness and the Mount Rose Wilderness.

Hike with others. Even on one-mile walks to a nearby waterfall, find at least one other person to hike with you. If your plans call for hiking at least five hours away from human habitation, go with two other people, and if you're hiking into a wilderness area, your group should ideally be made up of at least four people, but no more than 12. That way, if someone is hurt, one person can stay with the injured party while two others go for help.

In Yosemite National Park, anyone who stays in the backcountry overnight must have a wilderness permit, which is available free at any of several wilderness centers around the park. The permits let the park service monitor use of backcountry camps and make sure hikers are aware of any restrictions that may apply. In the national forests around Lake Tahoe, a wilderness permit is required for anyone who enters a designated wilderness area—a roadless area protected under federal law—whether he or she plans to spend the night or not. Permits can be filled out at the trailhead.

Before setting out on a hike, check the weather forecast. Tell someone where you are going and when you expect to be back. Take your cell phone. The reception can be surprisingly good in the High Sierra, particularly on high ridges or lakes, making search and rescue operations easier than ever before. (Just make sure you've recharged

OPPOSITE: San Harbor, Lake Tahoe–Nevada State Park.

the battery!) Leave your number with the same person you leave your route plans with.

Rangers will tell you that even on a short hike each group member should pack water, water purifying tablets, food in a bear-resistant canister, extra clothing, adhesive bandages or moleskin, sunglasses, a pocket knife, a whistle, any prescription medicines you may require, an extra pair of prescription glasses, an emergency shelter (such as a bright-colored trash bags or lightweight plastic tarp and waterproof matches and fire starter). At least one person in the group should carry a complete first-aid kit, insect repellent, sunscreen, a flashlight with extra batteries and bulbs, toilet paper, a latrine shovel or baggies for solid waste, a watch, pens and paper, an emergency kit containing a topographical map and compass, a metal mirror, 20 to 25 feet of nylon rope, and an emergency signaling device.

If you're going to be gone longer than a day trip, you'll also need lightweight cooking utensils, a lightweight stove and extra fuel, a tent, a sleeping bag, a ground cloth, a backpack and rain cover, more food, toiletries, more extra clothing, playing cards, a book . . . and maybe that electric wok. Hikers are routinely advised that their backpacks and gear should not exceed one-third of their body weight, which suggests that you may want to take the official recommended list with a grain of salt and consider what's really important. Otherwise, you may find yourself three miles up the trail, wondering why bears don't have to carry all this stuff.

camping

Most of the campgrounds in the Yosemite and Lake Tahoe areas are operated by the National Park Service, the National Forest Service, California or Nevada state parks or municipalities. Very few of them offer motorhome utility hookups—electricity, water or sewer. Some have dumping stations where RVs can empty their sewage holding tanks on the way out. Some campgrounds have limits on the length of motorhomes or trailers they can accommodate.

Very few campgrounds around Yosemite or Lake Tahoe operate on a first-come, first-served basis. At most of them, you're wise to make reservations. The exception is that on some fishing lakes that are packed with anglers on weekends, you may be lucky enough to find the extra-large campgrounds almost deserted during the week. Here's where to call to reserve a site at a public campground: **Yosemite National Park** (7 a.m. and 7 p.m.; 800-436-7275; reservations.nps.gov), **National Forest Service campgrounds** (877-444-6777; www.reservelcx3.com) and **California State Parks** (800-444-7275; www.reserveamerica.com).

Campgrounds open in April, May or June, depending on their elevation, and may remain open through Labor Day weekend at higher elevations or through mid-October at lower ones. A few, such as Lake Tahoe's Sugar Pine Point State Park, Tahoe Valley and Zephyr Cove, remain open year-round.

lodging & dining

Yosemite National Park has an amazing array of accommodations and price ranges, though there are fewer guest rooms in total than at the largest of the highrise Lake Tahoe casino resorts. At the low end of the Yosemite spectrum are woodframe canvas "camping cabins" and three-sided concrete cabins with canvas roofs and dividers and a privacy fence in place of the fourth wall—the kind of lodgings people used to live in during the Gold Rush, but today wouldn't meet municipal housing codes in California. At the other end, the Ahwahnee Hotel was built to meet the standards of European nobility and today maintains its rank as one of the world's finest small hotels.

Lodge at Tenaya.

Around Lake Tahoe, nothing can compete with the back-country elegance of the Ahwahnee or the subsistence-level accommodations at Yosemite's camping cabins and housekeeping cabins, but there's a wonderful array of lodging options. You could experience the vintage hotel at Historic Camp Richardson, relax amid a the small, comfortable cluster of rustic cabins secluded among the lodgepole pines along the North Shore, or check into one of the towering casino resorts across the lake at Stateline. In presenting the array of options, I use relative price ranges that let you compare the more-or-less costs at different places. These price ranges are based on the high-season (summer in Yosemite, summer or winter in Lake Tahoe) rate for a double. Room rates may be significantly lower in spring or fall, and some places have large suites with more features such as fireplaces, jacuzzis or balconies at much higher rates. Rate structures may change frequently.

As this edition goes to press, the relative room rate categories for Yosemite, Lake Tahoe and points in between are: ***budget***—less than $60 a night for two people; ***moderate***—$60 to $120 a night; ***deluxe***—$120 to $175 a night; and ***ultra-deluxe***—more than $175 a night (in a few instances, *much* more).

In both Yosemite and Lake Tahoe, especially in the small cottage complexes along Tahoe's North Shore, tipping the housekeepers is a graceful gesture and a step toward world peace.

The same situation that characterizes Yosemite and Lake Tahoe lodgings also applies to restaurants. At Yosemite, there's a complete range of dining alternatives, from fast-food, frozen yogurt and cafeteria cuisine to romantic candlelit gourmet dinners. None of them exactly compete with the others, and between them is something for everybody.

Lake Tahoe also has its share of fine dining, including the elegant top-floor at Stateline's tallest casino hotels as well as small restaurants in old North Shore houses, where independent-minded chefs present gourmet fare served with a Lake Tahoe sunset as a backdrop. The North Shore also has more than its share of cute little cafés and breakfast nooks. Curiously, almost all of the national fran-

OPPOSITE: Cooling off in the Tuolumne River.

Baldwin Beach, South Lake Tahoe.

chises are also located in the Stateline casinos. If you crave the reassuring familiarity of Subway, Planet Hollywood or the Hard Rock Café, you're most likely to find it in the big casino hotels, along with moderately priced all-you-can-eat buffets whose quality has come a long way in recent years to offer an array of irresistible California and international dishes to those who don't mind standing in line.

The relative price categories for restaurants in Yosemite and Lake Tahoe usually reflect the lowest-priced dinner entrées. Cafés that only serve breakfast and maybe lunch are categorized according to the lowest full-meal price on their menu: ***budget***—$9 or less; ***moderate***—$9 to $18; ***deluxe***—$18 to $25; and ***ultra-deluxe***—more than $25. In most budget restaurants, the entrée price and the tip are all you need to consider. In ultra-deluxe places, there are $15 appetizers, carafes of unbelievably good (well worth it) wine and accordingly large tips, so it's best to savor these dining experiences and realize that "more than $25" per person might mean $300 for you and a date.

kids

Both Yosemite and Lake Tahoe are among the most family-friendly places in California. Yosemite National Park, the forest service's Tahoe Basin Management Unit and some California State Parks around Lake Tahoe offer special children's activity programs.

In winter, many ski areas have slopes especially for young children and snowboard terrain parks for teens. Even the major gambling resorts on the Nevada side of Lake Tahoe free their guests to visit the casino—where minors are not allowed—by providing day-care centers, activity centers and video game arcades.

If you're planning to devote your visit to family hiking, start with a short, easy trail and learn your children's present walking rates. It takes longer—sometimes *much* longer—to hike the same distance with children. They have shorter strides. They often tend to expend a lot of energy quickly and run short of stamina, and they can distract themselves and you with the most interesting observations of nature. Bring plenty of sunscreen, insect repellent and snacks. Avoid edgy areas and those with large rock formations tempting to young climbers, and know where your kids are at all times.

pets

Dogs are not allowed on any backcountry trails in Yosemite National Park, though the park does offer kennel accommodations for a daily fee. In the national forests that surround both Yosemite and Lake Tahoe, dogs are welcome to run free except in campgrounds and trails with signs that say leashes are required, but at Lake Tahoe, dogs are prohibited on all public beaches on the California side and all but the hardest to reach on the Nevada side. Most, but not all, campgrounds in both areas allow pets. Small North Shore cabin complexes usually accept pets and may have an extra charge or a pet deposit requirement. Dogs are not accepted at most large resort hotels, including the big ski lodges at Squaw Valley and the Stateline casinos (except Harrah's, which takes small pets).

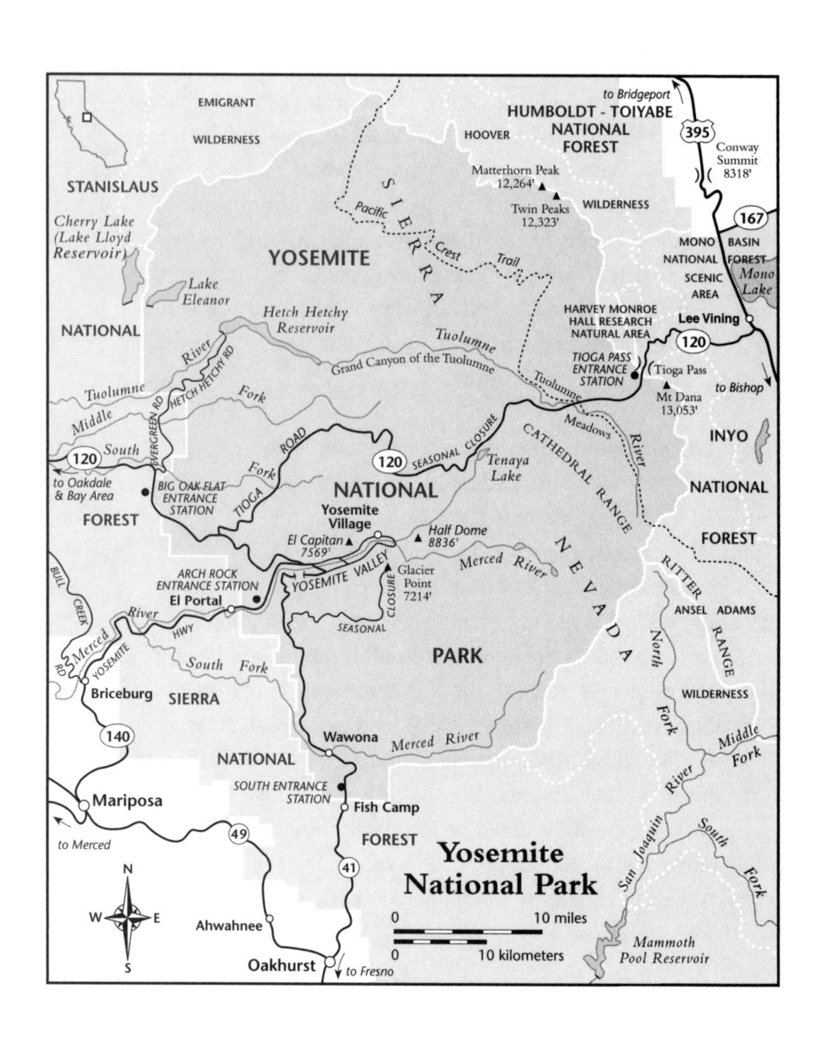
Yosemite National Park
EMIGRANT
WILDERNESS
STANISLAUS
Cherry Lake (Lake Lloyd Reservoir)
Lake Eleanor
NATIONAL
FOREST
HUMBOLDT - TOIYABE NATIONAL FOREST
HOOVER
WILDERNESS
Matterhorn Peak 12,264'
Twin Peaks 12,323'
to Bridgeport
395
Conway Summit 8318'
167
MONO BASIN NATIONAL FOREST SCENIC AREA
Mono Lake
Lee Vining
120
to Bishop
HARVEY MONROE HALL RESEARCH NATURAL AREA
TIOGA PASS ENTRANCE STATION
Tioga Pass
Mt Dana 13,053'
INYO
NATIONAL
FOREST
SIERRA NEVADA
Pacific Crest Trail
YOSEMITE
NATIONAL
PARK
Hetch Hetchy Reservoir
Tuolumne
Grand Canyon of the Tuolumne
Tuolumne Meadows
Tuolumne River
Middle Tuolumne River
HETCH HETCHY RD
EVERGREEN RD
South Fork
TIOGA ROAD
SEASONAL CLOSURE
Tenaya Lake
CATHEDRAL RANGE
120
to Oakdale & Bay Area
BIG OAK FLAT ENTRANCE STATION
Yosemite Village
El Capitan 7569'
Half Dome 8836'
Glacier Point 7214'
Merced River
YOSEMITE VALLEY
SEASONAL CLOSURE
ARCH ROCK ENTRANCE STATION
El Portal
BULL CREEK RD
Merced River
YOSEMITE HWY
South Fork
Briceburg
SIERRA
NATIONAL
FOREST
140
RITTER RANGE
ANSEL ADAMS
WILDERNESS
North Fork
Middle Fork
San Joaquin River
South Fork
Wawona
Merced River
SOUTH ENTRANCE STATION
Fish Camp
Mariposa
to Merced
49
41
N
W
E
S
Ahwahnee
Oakhurst
to Fresno
0
10 miles
0
10 kilometers
Mammoth Pool Reservoir

PART 1

California's Icon: Yosemite National Park

"The Yosemite Valley is a noble mark for the traveler, whether tourist, botanist, geologist or lover of wilderness pure and simple," wrote Sierra Club founder John Muir in *The Century Magazine* (the *19th* century, that is). "The walls of the valley are made up of rocks, mountains in size, separated from each other by side cañons and gorges; and they are so sheer in front, and so compactly and harmoniously built together on a level floor, that the place looks like some immense hall or temple lighted from above. But no temple made with hands can compare with Yosemite. Every rock in its walls seems to glow with life."

When Muir first arrived in 1868, parts of Yosemite had already been set aside as the first state park in America. Locals were baffled by the young journalist from Indiana who seemed to be squandering his talents by working for

a pittance as a shepherd and later a sawyer in a lumber mill. Yet in his spare time, Muir seized every opportunity to explore the wild backcountry and write about it, presenting a view of nature's interconnections that was utterly novel in his day. His words persuaded President Grover Cleveland to reserve a vast expanse of wilderness all the way to the eastern spine of the Sierra. Yosemite would become the prototype for almost all present-day national parks.

Today Yosemite continues to offer something to please and inspire just about every visitor. Those whose idea of a great time is a gentle stroll with the kids among big oak trees alive with chattering squirrels and scolding jays will find it here, with ice cream cones afterwards. It's equally feasible to climb a sheer cliff so tall and technically challenging that it takes two days and requires an overnight bivouac hanging from a windswept face a thousand feet above the citizenry in their cabins and campers. A stay in a world-class luxury hotel, complete with elegant gourmet meals, can be arranged. You can sit back and ride the free sightseeing tram through a grove of the world's largest trees or spend a week trekking between wilderness camps in the alpine high country. You can take a horseback ride to a spectacular waterfall or a camera safari in the footsteps of master photographer Ansel Adams, hit the slopes at California's oldest ski area or . . . how about a round of golf? It's all here, courtesy of Mother Nature and the National Park Service.

Although the wealth of recreational activities—and four million visitors each year—can sometimes make Yosemite seem like a huge theme park, the amazing fact is that it's also one of the best-preserved natural areas in California, thanks largely to the U.S. government's rigid protective regulations. Today, the greatest challenge facing Yosemite is the impact of the large numbers of motor vehicles that jam its roads in the summer months. An 800-page plan proposed by the park service in 1980 and stalled by controversies and litigation ever since envisions banning all cars from the park and limiting traffic to public shuttles. When or whether this will actually happen is uncertain, but the Yosemite Area Regional Transportation System (YARTS) has already come into existence, not only carrying visitors to and from trailheads throughout the park but also bringing them in from park-and-ride stations as far away as the towns of El Portal, Merced and Mammoth Lake.

One thing is certain. Change is in the wind at Yosemite. There has never been a better time than now to visit this magnificent national park—if only so you can look back in future years and say, "I remember the way it was back when . . . ."

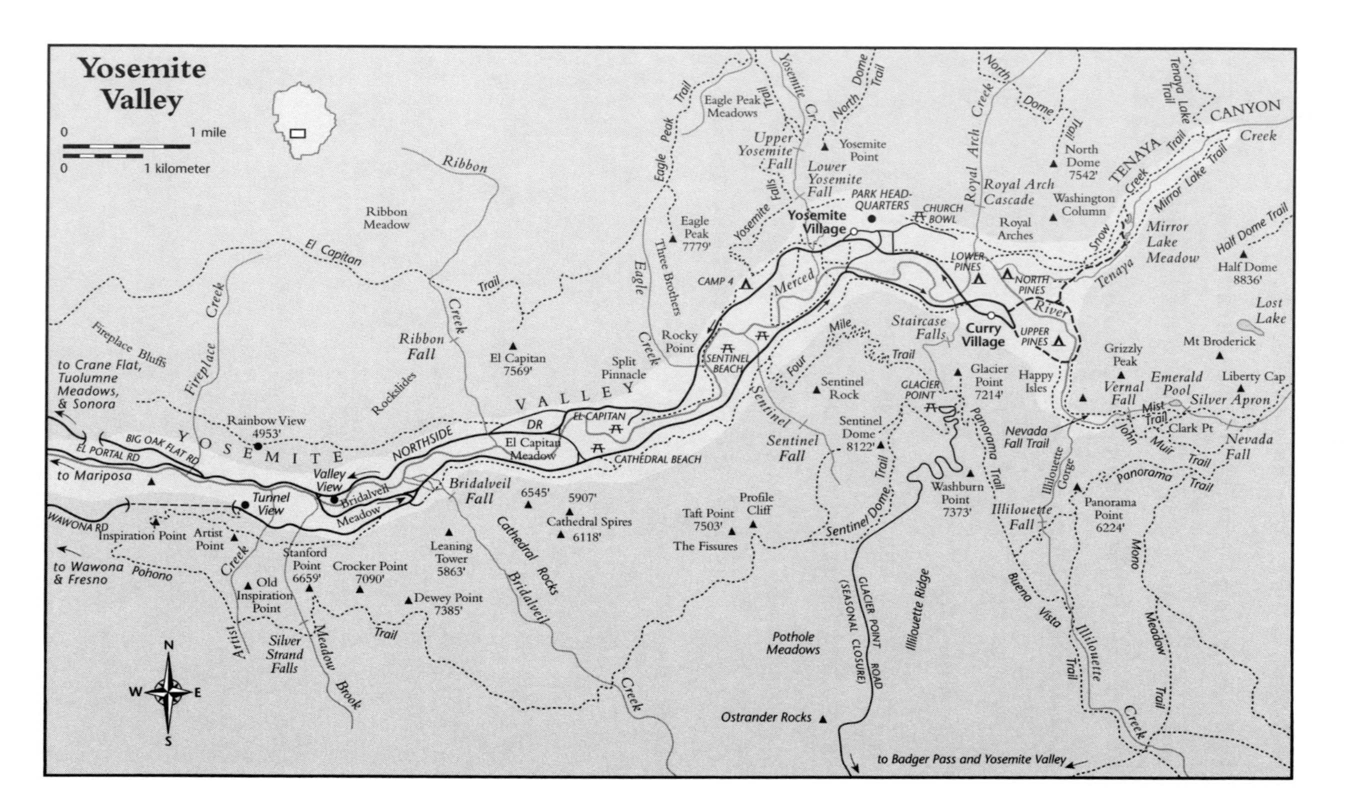

Yosemite Valley
0
1 mile
0
1 kilometer
Ribbon
Ribbon Meadow
El Capitan
Trail
Creek
Ribbon Fall
El Capitan 7569'
Fireplace Bluffs
Fireplace
Creek
to Crane Flat, Tuolumne Meadows, & Sonora
Rockslides
Rainbow View 4953'
YOSEMITE
VALLEY
BIG OAK FLAT RD
EL PORTAL RD
to Mariposa
NORTHSIDE
DR
EL CAPITAN
El Capitan Meadow
CATHEDRAL BEACH
Valley View
Bridalveil
Meadow
Tunnel View
WAWONA RD
Inspiration Point
Artist Point
Creek
to Wawona & Fresno
Pohono
Old Inspiration Point
Artist
Silver Strand Falls
Meadow
Brook
Stanford Point 6659'
Crocker Point 7090'
Dewey Point 7385'
Trail
Leaning Tower 5863'
Bridalveil Fall
6545'
5907'
Cathedral Spires 6118'
Cathedral
Rocks
Bridalveil
Creek
Eagle Peak Trail
Eagle Peak Meadows
Trail
Eagle Peak 7779'
Three Brothers
Eagle
Creek
Rocky Point
Split Pinnacle
CAMP 4
SENTINEL BEACH
Upper Yosemite Fall
Yosemite Cr.
Yosemite Falls
North Dome Trail
Yosemite Point
Lower Yosemite Fall
Yosemite Village
PARK HEAD-QUARTERS
CHURCH BOWL
Royal Arch Creek
North
Dome
Trail
Royal Arch Cascade
Royal Arches
North Dome 7542'
Washington Column
TENAYA
Creek
Trail
Tenaya Lake Trail
CANYON
Creek
Mirror Lake Trail
Mirror Lake Meadow
Snow
Tenaya
Half Dome Trail
Half Dome 8836'
Lost Lake
Merced
River
LOWER PINES
NORTH PINES
UPPER PINES
Curry Village
Four
Mile
Trail
Staircase Falls
Sentinel Rock
Sentinel
Sentinel Fall
Sentinel Dome 8122'
GLACIER POINT
Glacier Point 7214'
Happy Isles
Panorama
Trail
Washburn Point 7373'
Taft Point 7503'
Profile Cliff
The Fissures
Sentinel Dome
Trail
GLACIER POINT ROAD
(SEASONAL CLOSURE)
Illilouette Ridge
Pothole Meadows
Ostrander Rocks
to Badger Pass and Yosemite Valley
Grizzly Peak
Vernal Fall
Emerald Pool
Mt Broderick
Liberty Cap
Silver Apron
Mist Trail
John Muir Trail
Clark Pt
Nevada Fall
Nevada Fall Trail
Illilouette Gorge
Illilouette Fall
Panorama Point 6224'
Panorama Trail
Buena Vista Trail
Illilouette
Creek
Mono
Meadow
Trail
N
W
E
S

2

Yosemite Valley

Wrapped in a wonderland of waterfalls that plunge over precipitous rock faces, guarded by granite domes and filled with black oak and incense cedar, the hidden paradise of Yosemite Valley is absolutely unique. Through more than a century of Spanish colonialism in California, the valley remained unknown, the secret home of the Ahwahnee people. Discovered by outsiders just a year after California became a state, Yosemite Valley became one of California's leading tourist destinations almost immediately and remains so today. With nearly 4,000,000 people a year passing through its gates, Yosemite ranks as one of the top five most visited national parks in the United States, and virtually every visitor starts his or her adventure at Yosemite Valley. In fact, some people hardly explore beyond the valley—and why should they? Where else can you find great hiking, rock climbing, horseback riding, gentle river rafting and biking—not to mention world-class dining and lodging—all within an area of only seven square miles?

sightseeing

As you approach Yosemite Valley by road for the first time, you may experience a feeling of awe mixed with a touch of dèjá vu, for, like the Grand Canyon or Yellowstone's Old Faithful Geyser, the valley's giant domes form one of the most instantly recognizable views in the American West. The road enters the valley through what 19th-century romantic artists called the Gates of Yosemite—the sheer walls of **El Capitan**, a monolith twice the size of the Rock of Gibraltar. Pause for a look at the daredevil rock climbers who can be seen inching their way up the cliffs.

THE REAL GRIZZLY ADAMS

Three years after the first non-Indians found Yosemite, trapper James Capen Adams came to capture grizzly bears, which were abundant in those days. He trained them to perform in Wild West shows and became famous as "Grizzly" Adams (no relation to Ansel!).

On your right across the road, **Leaning Tower** seems to tilt impossibly to the west, two million pounds of rock threatening (as it has for 10,000 years or more) to topple at any minute. Nearby **Cathedral Spires**, a cluster of jagged peaks whose majesty, surpassing that of Notre Dame or Chartres, must have inspired in early visitors to the valley a palpable sense of the presence of God—as it still does for many of us today.

As you enter the valley, you may wonder why it's not called a canyon instead. "Valley" seems too mild a term for a gorge that is at once claustrophobic and vast, running ten miles along the **Merced River** between sheer vertical cliffs of cream-colored granite that rise as much as 3500 feet—as high, in many places, as the valley is wide.

El Capitan.

Just before you pass between El Capitan and Cathedral Spires, the park road splits into a one-way loop. **Southside Drive** follows the south bank of the river upcanyon, then crosses the river and returns downcanyon as **Northside Drive**. Unless traffic is exceptionally heavy, it's a good idea to start with an orientation drive all the way around the loop, identifying each place you may want to drive to later in your stay, since if you miss a picnic ground or trailhead parking area you'll have to drive the slow ten-mile circuit again to get back to it.

On your left, across the road from the base of Cathedral Spires, a short road turns off to **Cathedral Beach**, a picnic area with restrooms and swimming. As you continue, an unbroken wall of rock rises on your right, and if you crane your neck to look skyward, you can make out **Taft Point**, one of several promontories above the valley that can be reached from other parts of the park.

The next major landmark on your right is **Sentinel Rock**, a massive, bare cliff that divides as it rises to form a row of castlelike towers more than 3000 feet above the valley floor. Here you'll find a trailhead for Four Mile Trail to the top rim at **Glacier Point**.

Across the road is **Sentinel Beach**, another riverside picnic area with parking, restrooms and swimming; it serves as the pullout point for rafting, kayaking, canoeing and tubing in the valley. A short distance farther along is another developed picnic area beside the **Swinging Bridge** on the valley's bicycle path.

A little farther up the road on your right you'll see the **Yosemite Community Chapel**, where Protestant church services are held on Sundays and more than a thousand weddings are performed each year. ~ 209-372-4831. Across the road is the turnoff to the central day-use parking area. Continuing along Southside Drive, you'll pass **LeConte Memorial Lodge** on your right. The original park visitors center, the lodge is now operated by the Sierra Club as a children's activity center.

The end of Southside Drive brings you to one of the main service areas in the park. Here you'll find the **Curry Village** tent-cabin complex and short roadways to the Pines Campgrounds, the Nature Center at Happy Isles, Yosemite Valley Stables, the village's bike rental center and several trail-

EXPLORING WITHOUT A WINDSHIELD

Any mode of transportation that doesn't involve driving will let you better appreciate the exceptional natural beauty that surrounds Yosemite Village. Walking trails and paved bike paths go everywhere in the developed part of the valley, and free shuttles circle constantly among 21 stops in the valley, including Yosemite Lodge, the Ahwahnee Hotel, Curry Village, the Happy Isles Nature Center and the trailhead to Mirror Lake, as well as the central parking area and Yosemite Village.

First People of the Valley

The southern Miwok Indians led an apparently Edenlike existence in Yosemite Valley, unknown to the outside world until the mid-19th century. Besides moderate weather and abundant game, they had a virtually unlimited supply of acorns, which they ground into meal and used in much the same way that other native people used corn. They called their valley Ahwahnee ("valley like a gaping mouth") and referred to themselves as Ahwahneeche ("Ahwahnee people"). Perversely, the first U.S. soldiers to enter the valley, searching for Indians who had raided a trading post, immediately changed its name to the one by which neighboring Paiutes called the Ahwahneeche—Yosemite, which means "they sometimes kill people." The Army relocated the Ahwahneeche to a reservation near Fresno but let them return home to the valley that winter. When two prospectors were killed the following year, allegedly by Indians, the Ahwahneeche moved down from the mountains to live at Mono Lake with the Paiutes, who spoke a different language, had different customs and ate different food—brine shrimp and fly larvae. After the Ahwahneeche chief was killed in a dispute with the Paiutes, some Ahwahneeche left the area to join other Miwok bands, while others eventually returned to Yosemite to become one of the new park's tourist attractions.

An umacha, *a traditional Ahwahneeche structure made of bark.*

Today, many Miwok have joined California's multicultural mainstream. More traditional descendants of the Ahwahneeche live at Tuolumne Ranchería, a small Indian reservation off Route 108 northeast of the park, where the annual Mi-Wuk Indian Acorn Festival is held in September. A few Indian families continue to make their homes in Yosemite National Park as employees of the park service.

heads. Also flanking Yosemite Valley is the gracefully curved south side of **Half Dome**, which dominates the entirety of Yosemite Valley with angular chiseled north faces rising so sheer that hardly a hand- or foothold can be detected.

From Curry Village, the park road crosses the river and turns back downcanyon to become **Northside Drive**. Just before you reach the central day-use parking area again, a road turns off to the right, then right again, past the famous **Ahwahnee Hotel**

Half Dome.

and below the even more magnificent **Royal Arches** formation, a gigantic rainbow of rock.

Returning from the Ahwahnee brings you back to the tourist heart of the valley, **Yosemite Village**. Either now or after you've completed your orientation drive, park in the big, free central parking lot between the auto repair garage and the main village.

Yosemite Village is a row of rustic and modern buildings that includes restaurants and the **Village Store**, which sells groceries, camping supplies and a wide selection of curios. The **Ansel Adams Gallery** exhibits and sells prints of works by the master photographer who immortalized Yosemite in black and white. ~ 209-372-4413.

JUST FOR KIDS

The Sierra Club presents nature programs for children at the **LeConte Memorial Lodge** between 10 a.m. and 4 p.m. Wednesday through Sunday from June to mid-September. Hands-on kids' activities are also offered at the **Happy Isles Nature Center** from mid-June to late September. For current programs, consult the free *Yosemite Today* newspaper you receive when entering the park.

In the middle of the village, the **Visitors Center** has an information desk where park rangers can help you plan for hikes and other activities. (If your plans include an overnight or longer trek into the backcountry, check in next door at the Wilderness

Center, where you can get a permit as well as advice and rent a bear-resistant food canister.) The Visitors Center also has interpretive displays that demonstrate with three-dimensional models how geological events created Yosemite Valley and identify local plants and wildlife through panoramic paintings, taxidermy and touch-me exhibits. There's also a regionally oriented bookstore. ~ 209-372-0200; www.nps.gov/yose.

Past the Visitors Center, the **Indian Cultural Museum** contains basketry and other artifacts of the Ahwahneeche people, the southern Miwok Indian tribe that lived in Yosemite until they were relocated in the late 19th century. Behind the museum building is a re-creation of an Ahwahneeche village with *umachas* (conical huts made of tree bark), an earth-covered chief's house and a community longhouse.

The walking and biking path between Yosemite Village and the main parking area continues westward across Yosemite Creek to the base of **Yosemite Falls**, perhaps the most awe-inspiring of the waterfalls that surround the valley. Split into a 320-foot lower fall, a steeply slanted 675-foot middle cascade,

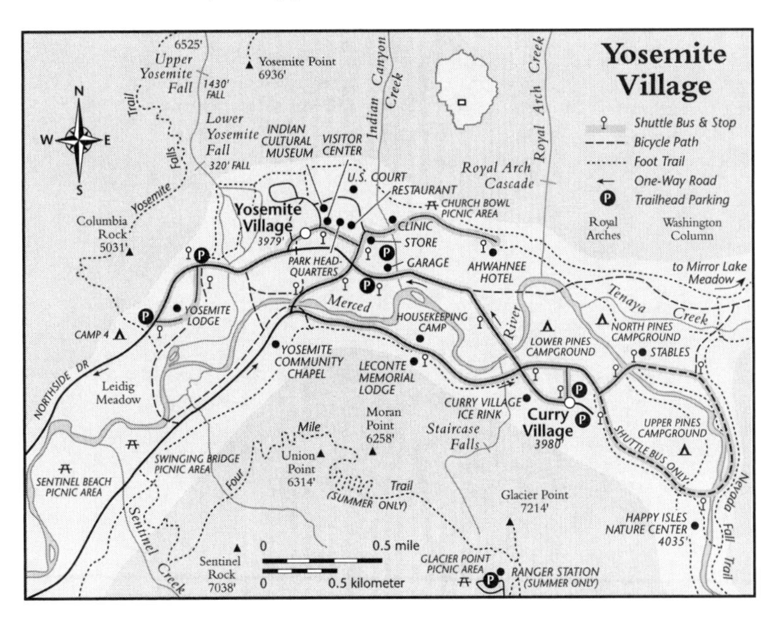

You Gotta Have Art

Ever since the 1940s, the park service has sponsored free art programs for visitors who want to learn ways of capturing Yosemite's natural beauty. At the **Art Activity Center** in Yosemite Village, guest artists present workshops in sketching, watercolor painting and other artforms from 10:30 a.m. to 2 p.m. in spring, summer and fall, first-come, first-served. The **Ansel Adams Gallery** offers guided camera walks most mornings—sign up at the gallery or any hotel tour desk in the park. ~ 209-372-4413. The Yosemite Association has a **Field Seminar Program** that conducts multiday outdoor workshops. ~ 209-379-2646.

For those who wish to remain spectators, the **Museum Gallery** in Yosemite Village exhibits a collection of works by 19th- and 20th-century artists who painted Yosemite landscapes.

and a 1430-foot upper fall, it's one of the valley's most familiar landmarks. From here, you get just enough of a view of the falls to challenge you to try the half-day hike to the top—a grueling climb, for sure, but one that will let you claim you've climbed a cliff in Yosemite even if you don't know a piton from a carabiner. The falls are best viewed in the morning, when the sunlight strikes them most directly, and especially in late spring, when the creek that feeds the falls is swollen with snowmelt; however, the sight of them is sure to impress even the most jaded visitor at any time of day and year.

Now that your car is parked in the central parking lot, your best bet is to leave it there unless you have a hotel or campground reservation. There are a host of adventures to be had in Yosemite Valley, and none of them involves driving a car.

outdoor adventures

When you consider that nearly 1600 individuals, couples and families stay in Yosemite Valley every night during high season, it should come as no surprise that participating in outdoor activities in the valley can seem a lot like visiting Disneyland—busy, unbelievably crowded and, at the end of the day, well worth it. Yet even here, hikers will discover that the vast majority of visitors lack enthusiasm for walking a mile or more away from a paved road or trail. By choosing a more ambitious hike, you can es-

Opposite: Yosemite Falls.

cape the throngs of casual sightseers. Of course, if you're a rock climber, you can find solitude on the sheer face of El Capitan or Sentinel Rock—as long as you don't look down. If you do, you'll realize that you've become a tourist "sight" yourself!

HIKING

Everywhere you cast your gaze in Yosemite Valley, the scenery tantalizes you to put on your hiking boots and explore it up close. Of course, at any given moment, a thousand or more visitors are entertaining the same idea. The longer and steeper the trail you choose, the more likely you are to escape the crowds. For real solitude, you'll need to head out into the other 99.4 percent of the park area outside of Yosemite Valley. But before you do, take time to experience the majesty of Yosemite Valley on some of these great walks and discover what makes this special spot so popular. Distances listed are one way unless otherwise noted.

You can walk the length of the valley on the six-mile **Merced River Trail**. For much of the way, foot trails run along both sides of the river with minimal elevation gain. The easy walk along the unmarked but wide and obvious trail extends from the canyon mouth between the sheer cliffs of El Capitan

The Man Who Shot Yosemite

Although painters like Albert Bierstadt and Thomas Moran depicted the landscapes of Yosemite in the 1800s, the artist who introduced most Americans to the park's natural beauty was Ansel Adams (1902—84), one of the 20th century's most renowned photographers. Born in San Francisco, Adams dropped out of school at age 13 and was educated by private tutors. The following year, his family took him to Yosemite for the first time—an experience that he claimed led to his final career choice. Aspiring to become a professional musician, Adams did not try his hand at photography until age 25. When he did, he took to cameras and film with near-fanatical enthusiasm and soon returned to Yosemite to learn his craft in the most photogenic setting possible. His reputation was secured five years later when he invented a technique called tonal exposure, which allowed greater contrast, gray-scale range and special effects in black-and-white photography.

Although Adams photographed many subjects, including the Mormons of Utah for a *Life* magazine photo essay, his main passion was always Yosemite. He taught the first Yosemite art workshop in 1940 with fellow photographer Edward Weston and continued to teach there throughout his life. He received three Guggenheim grants to photograph America's national parks.

Adams served as chairman of the board of directors of the Sierra Club for 37 years and founded the Friends of Photography, which operates the Ansel Adams Center for Photography in San Francisco.

and Cathedral Rocks to the place where Tenaya Creek flows into the river and the trail splits, one fork going to Mirror Lake and the other to Happy Isles Nature Center and Vernal Fall.

Another easy walk follows the bridle trail (watch where you step!) from the front gate of the **Ahwahnee Hotel to Yosemite Lodge**, a distance of about 1.5 miles, with free shuttle stops at both ends. Leading among large oak trees, the trail makes a short descent to cross a bridge at the foot of Yosemite Falls, affording a spectacular view of the 320-foot lower fall.

Whether by the Ahwahnee Hotel to Yosemite Lodge trail or the more direct route from the parking area across the road from Yosemite Lodge to the bridge and back, walking to the foot of Yosemite Falls is easy. Experiencing the falls in their full glory is more challenging. One of the first trails in the park designed especially for tourists, the 3.3-mile **Yosemite Falls Trail** was built in the 1870s by the management of the first hotel in the valley and originally had an admission fee. The trailhead is at Camp 4. Since there is no parking unless you're staying at the campground, take the free shuttle from the main parking area to stop number 7. The first leg of this strenuous half-day hike climbs a series of switchbacks through oak forest, putting more than one-fourth of the 2000-foot altitude gain behind you in the first half-mile as it ascends to Columbia Rock, with its grand vista of the valley below. Soon after, 1430-foot Upper Yosemite Fall comes into view for the first time. From there on, the huge fall is almost constantly in view. Beyond the overlook at the top of the fall, the trail splits twice and continues to **Porcupine Flat** (6 miles), **Yosemite Creek Campground** (6 miles) and **Tamarack Flat** (11.8 miles), all on the Tioga Road.

If you have time for only one hike—and you're not accompanied by small children—don't miss the dramatic ascent of the **Yosemite Falls Trail**. From the vista point at the top, you'll see for yourself why this was Yosemite's first trail built especially for tourists.

The most popular hike in the valley is the easy and often congested **Mirror Lake Trail**, one mile each way through pine and fir forest with a 100-foot altitude gain. Start at the trailhead at shuttle stop number 17 near Valley Stables; parking is available nearby at Curry Village. Mirror Lake came into be-

ing when a rockfall blocked Tenaya Creek, creating a swampy meadow that park workers enhanced in 1890 with a manmade dam. The park service stopped maintaining the dam in 1971. The famous photogenic reflective pool is now gradually leaking away and only fills up during the spring runoff. Some maps now label it "Mirror Meadow." A short, self-guiding nature trail loops around the west shoreline of the seasonal lake. You can also make the Mirror Lake hike into a three-mile loop trip by returning on the longer, paved bicycle road.

The **Mist Trail**, which climbs 3.7 miles to Vernal Fall and Nevada Fall, starts at the Happy Isles Nature Center near Upper Pines Campground. Take the free valley shuttle from the main parking area to stop number 16, or park in the trailhead parking area near Curry Village. After a mile, the moderately strenuous trail descends to Vernal Bridge. A little farther on, the John Muir Trail intersects the Mist Trail for the first of several times along the route; remember this trail junction—you may wish to take the alternate trail on your return trip. Soon after, 300 slippery steps ascend the cliff face through the waterfall spray for which the Mist Trail was named, finally reaching a viewpoint near the brink of 317-foot Vernal Fall. (Hiking boots or athletic shoes that grip well are a must on this hike, and a lightweight waterproof jacket may come in handy.) Another half-mile brings you to Clark Point, which affords the best vista of Vernal Fall. Beyond, 594-foot Nevada Fall comes into view. A short, steep switchback climb takes you to the top of the fall, where a bridge crosses the Merced River and a side trail descends to the brink of the fall. Most day-hikers start back at this point. Many hikers take a short segment of the John Muir Trail on the return trip to bypass Vernal Fall, since the wet rock steps are more dangerous to descend than to climb.

THE TRAIL JOHN MUIR BLAZED

The **John Muir Trail**, which starts at the Happy Isles trailhead in Yosemite Valley, extends 211 miles south to Mount Whitney. Except for this first segment, from the valley to Tuolumne Meadows, most of the trail is now incorporated in the Canada-to-Mexico Pacific Crest Trail. The first four miles of the John Muir Trail is used for guided half-day horseback rides to Nevada Falls. The complete trek to Mount Whitney takes approximately 30 days.

The trail beyond Nevada Fall is the most popular one in the Yosemite Valley area for overnight or longer backpacking trips. If you continue beyond the fall, it takes you three miles to **Little Yosemite Valley**, where there's a backpackers' campground (caution: Bears like it, too), then 14 more miles to Tuolumne Meadows (see Chapter 4), where the John Muir Trail merges with the Pacific Crest Trail. Another strenuous trail from Little Yosemite Valley goes two miles north to **Half Dome**, the 8836-foot giant that looms above Mirror Lake.

Four Mile Trail runs from the trailhead on South Valley Road to Glacier Point. The strenuous, though amazingly scenic, route, open in summer only, ascends 3600 feet in elevation in just 4.6 miles. (It was originally four miles long, hence the name, but was later rerouted to avoid a treacherously steep segment, making it somewhat longer.) Along the way, it skirts the base of Sentinel Rock and pauses midway at Union Point for a view of the valley and Yosemite Falls. Of course, you can drive to Glacier Point, a roundabout trip that takes nearly an hour (see Chapter 3). Better yet, for a small fee you can catch one of the hikers' buses that run between the valley and Glacier Point daily from June through September for a one-way, half-day hike either uphill or downhill. The descent sounds easier, but because of the steep switchback segments the downhill hike will leave your leg muscles sorer. The buses make pick-up stops at Yosemite Lodge, the Ahwahnee Hotel and Curry Village. Reservations are advisable. ~ 209-372-1240.

ROCK CLIMBING

With its near-vertical walls of high-quality granite, Yosemite is one of the world's great technical climbing meccas. There are outstanding climbs to be found in other

To Climb the Unclimbable Rock

When he saw Half Dome, the rock that looms 4000 feet straight up above Mirror Lake, 19th-century geologist Josiah Whitney declared it "probably the only one of all the prominent points in Yosemite which never has been and never will be trodden by human foot." Just five years later, retired blacksmith George Anderson proved him wrong, not only climbing the 900-foot back side of Half Dome but drilling holes and inserting eye bolts to anchor ropes that would make the climb easier for future hikers. Later the Sierra Club replaced the bolts and ropes with waist-high poles and steel cables to form a railing for climbers. Today more than a hundred people climb Half Dome each day during the summer months. In August 2002, Cliff Hiemforth made the strenuous 8.5-mile hike to Half Dome and climbed to the top of the rock at the age of 82—the oldest person on record to make the ascent.

areas of the park, but nothing can compare to the big faces that surround Yosemite Valley. It's here that most state-of-the-art climbing gear and modern climbing techniques were originally developed. The climbing season is from April to October.

The most famous climbing area, **El Capitan** boasts more than 75 established routes up its faces to the summit, as well as an equal number of shorter and sometimes easier climbs. Some El Capitan ascent routes require the climber to bivouac for one or even two nights hanging on the sheer rock face. A wilderness permit is *not* required for an overnight stay on a climb.

Other routes go up just about every cliff around Yosemite Valley. A number of books available at the Visitors Center bookstore in Yosemite Village detail the possibilities. Most routes are Class IV, for expert climbers only, but there are a few Class I and II climbs that less experienced climbers can safely tackle. Among them are **Lower Cathedral Rock**, **Royal Arches** and some routes beside **Yosemite Falls**. Even some of the big crack climbs on **El Capitan** fall into this category.

Give Something Back: Conscious Climbing

Due to the number of climbers in Yosemite Valley, rock climbing has caused obvious environmental impacts including destruction of lichens and other cliffside vegetation, disturbance of cliff-dwelling wildlife, water pollution from improper human waste disposal, and unsightly litter, chalk marks and pin scars. You can help reduce this damage in several ways:

- Never toss or drop anything from a wall;
- Pick up any litter you see and carry it back down with you;
- Never leave food or water behind "for future parties";
- Carry a plastic container or "poop tube" for human waste;
- Never leave equipment on a cliff face;
- Avoid pushing soil downhill or walking on vegetation;
- Build fires only in established fire rings;
- Check the information kiosk at Camp 4 for peregrine falcon closures;
- Join or organize a volunteer group cleanup.

Statistically, rock climbing is by far the most dangerous outdoor activity in the park. More than 100 climbing accidents happen in Yosemite each year. The biggest danger is falling rocks or equipment. Other hazards include dehydration and hypothermia, as well as incompetent climbers and inadequate gear. In short, respect your personal limitations. Unless you're a topnotch climber, a visit to Yosemite may be a good opportunity to improve your skills with a lesson or a guided climb. Technical rock climbing lessons and guide service are offered by the **Yosemite Mountaineering School**. ~ 209-372-1000.

FISHING

Fishing is allowed in the Merced River and its tributaries, though most anglers will tell you that your chances of catching anything are slim to none because the park

service stopped stocking streams and lakes decades ago. Still, it's as good an excuse as any to sit quietly amid some of the most magnificent scenery on earth. California fishing regulations apply within the park, and people age 16 and older must have a valid California fishing license. The fishing season is from the last Saturday in April through November 15.

In Yosemite Valley, rainbow trout are catch-and-release only, and the limit for brown trout is five per day or ten in possession. Fishing from bridges is prohibited. Only artificial lures or flies with barbless hooks may be used. Possession of live or dead minnows or other bait fish, amphibians, fish eggs or roe is illegal in the park.

Fishing supplies and licenses are available at the **Yosemite Village Sport Shop** and the **Curry Village Mountain Shop**. ~ 209-372-0740.

HORSEBACK RIDING

Forget about galloping free with the wind in your face. In Yosemite Valley, horseback adventures are limited to guided trail rides, often in large groups. But once in the saddle, you can take one of the two-hour rides go to **Mirror Lake**. Four-hour rides ascend the John Muir Trail to **Nevada Fall**. Some all-day rides take Four Mile Trail up to **Glacier Point**, while others go to **Half Dome**. Reservations are necessary and can usually be made for the following day after you arrive in the park. Make reserva-

tions through your hotel's tour desk or call **Yosemite Valley Stables**. ~ 209-372-8348. The stables are located near North Pines Campground at valley shuttle stop number 18.

BIKING

One of the nicest ways to get around the valley is by bicycle. Twelve miles of flat, paved bike paths make their way around the developed part of Yosemite Valley, including an eight-mile loop, a shortcut that shortens the loop by two miles, and a spur that leads to the Mirror Lake trailhead. Bicycles are also allowed on all national park roads, paved or unpaved, that are open to motor vehicles. Bikes are prohibited on all backcountry trails.

You can rent fat-tire newspaper bikes at **Yosemite National Park Bike Rentals** in Curry Village. ~ 209-372-8319. More bikes from the same fleet are for rent at the **Yosemite Lodge Bike Stand**. ~ 209-372-1208. The bikes are rented for the day and can't be kept overnight.

RIVER RUNNING

There's nothing like floating down an ice-cold river in the heat of summer. Rafting, canoeing and kayaking on the calm Merced River are popular in June and July. These boats, as well as inner tubes and other floatation devices, are limited to the stretch of river between Stoneman Bridge near Curry Village and Sentinel Beach Picnic Area and only between 10 a.m. and 6 p.m. Rafts, life jackets and paddles are for rent at **Curry Village**. ~ 209-372-0740.

CAMPING

With the exception of one walk-in campground designed especially for rock climbers, camping in Yosemite Valley means parking your rig or pitching your tent in one of the three campgrounds set close together near Curry

Village. Their greatest virtue, other than the awe-inspiring scenery that surrounds them, is that they're within easy walking distance of just about anything your heart might desire while spending a night in the wilderness. The entrance for all three drive-in campgrounds in Yosemite Valley is located on the main road into the valley, just past Curry Village.

Upper Pines Campground has 238 tent/RV sites in six large camping loops. It's so big and busy that you may feel as if you haven't quite left the city behind. On the plus side, it's close to the Happy Isles trailhead, starting point for the Mist Trail. Green belts of live oak and cedar provide some semblance of privacy, and there's a neck-craning view of nearby Lambert Dome. There are restrooms, drinking water and a dump station, but no hookups. Sites cost $18 per night. Open year-round.

Lower Pines Campground is smaller than Upper Pines, with 60 tent/RV sites packed along the bank of the Merced River. Behind the campground, stands of oak and ponderosa with a walking path through them insulate the campsites from the busy road through Curry Village, where there are six free shuttle stops within easy walking distance. There are restrooms and drinking water, but no hookups. Sites cost $18 per night. Open March through October.

North Pines Campground, on the opposite bank of the river from Lower Pines, has 81 tent/RV sites. Situated at the conflu-

ence of Tenaya Creek and the Merced River, the campground has flowing water and lush riparian flora on three sides. The location is next to the riding stables and the busy Mirror Lake Trail. There are restrooms and drinking water, but no hookups. Sites cost $18 per night. Open April through September.

Camp 4 (formerly called Sunnyside Campground) is a walk-in campground designed for rock climbers planning early-morning ascents of El Capitan, which towers directly above the camp. The view, both upcanyon toward Half Dome and downcanyon toward El Capitan and Cathedral Rocks, is one of the best in the valley. Yosemite Falls is a short walk away on the trail that starts from Camp 4. Six people—whether they know each other or not—are assigned to each of the 35 tent sites, which generally means sharing a picnic table and campfire ring with strangers. Sites cost $5 per person, first-come, first-served. No pets. Open year-round. To get there, after entering Yosemite Valley, turn left at the first stop sign, drive .25 mile and turn left again at the next stop sign, then drive .5 mile and turn right at the sign marking the Camp 4 parking area.

If you're tenting and the main park campgrounds seem a little tame for your taste, check out **Camp 4**, where sharing a site with strangers often means an impromptu party with people who plan to risk their lives climbing rock cliffs in the morning.

Reservations are required for Upper Pines, Lower Pines and North Pines campgrounds, as well as for some campgrounds in other areas of the park outside Yosemite Valley. Reservations can be made four to five months in advance, starting on the 15th of the month. To make reservations, contact NPRS, P.O. Box 1600, Cumberland, MD 21502; 800-436-7275 between 7 a.m. and 7 p.m. Pacific Standard Time; or e-mail at reservations.nps.gov. Be sure to include the desired location (campground and, if you wish, site number) and the type of camping equipment (tent, RV, etc.). Payment is required at the time the reservation is made. There is a seven-day limit in the summer at all Yosemite Valley campgrounds, and camping within the park is limited to 30 days per year.

lodging

Beginning in the 1960s, the park service decided to reduce the number of accommodations in Yosemite National Park. Today many are temporary canvas structures that allow maximum flexibility for future lodging configurations. Barely a cut above camping, these units make a striking contrast with the Ahwahnee Hotel, one of the most elegant and atmospheric rustic luxury hotels anywhere. The 427 canvas tent cabins at **Curry**

Bears and Your Lunch

There's an excellent reason for the food storage "bear box" installed at each campsite in Yosemite National Park. During the late summer and early fall, an adult black bear must eat 20,000 calories per day to build up enough fat to survive the winter's hibernation. While it's possible to satisfy this kind of appetite with massive amounts of berries and acorns, Yosemite's bears have learned through many generations that the easiest place to find food is in tourists' tents, cars, backpacks or picnic baskets. Besides the danger to humans and their property, as a bear learns to depend on human food it may become aggressive. When that happens, park rangers must kill the bear—a tragedy that occurs almost every year.

Until recently, Yosemite National Park had about 1500 incidents each year in which bears confronted visitors, broke into their cars or raided their camping gear. In 1998, the park service installed the bear boxes in campsites and implemented new regulations that prohibit storing food in vehicles after dark, keeping food outside of bear boxes day or night in campgrounds or tent cabins, leaving hotel room or cabin windows open with food in the room, or leaving food unattended anywhere outdoors. Backpackers are required to carry all food in bear-resistant canisters, which can be rented at the Yosemite Valley Sports Shop, the Wilderness Center, or any of eight other locations in the park.

Since these regulations were adopted, the number of bear incidents has declined by 85 percent. Still, food raids by bears caused $30,000 in property damage in 2001. Most of the damage was to motor vehicles in the form of smashed windows or ripped doors. Protect your car: Use a bear box or canister and, when driving, carry as little food as possible.

Cabins at Curry Village.

Village are set on raised wood platforms and furnished with beds, linens and electric lights; they have no phones, electrical outlets, heat or plumbing and no maid service. The tent cabin area has two large central restrooms with showers. Curry Village also has 182 hard-sided cabins, most with two double beds and tables or dressers. All have electric lights and electric or propane heaters as well as daily maid service, but no phones or televisions. About half the cabins have private baths, while the others share nearby restrooms. In addition, 18 large, modern guest rooms are available in the central lodge, each with a private bath and most other standard motel amenities, but no telephones or televisions. Open April through October. ~ 209-372-8333, reservations 209-252-4848, fax 209-372-4816; www.yosemitepark.com. BUDGET TO MODERATE.

JUNIOR RANGERS

The Yosemite Association offers a **Junior Ranger** program for kids ages seven to thirteen. Parents buy an official booklet for $3.50 at any of the park's visitors centers. Those who complete the exercises in the booklet, participate in a ranger-guided activity and collect a bag of litter receive a Junior Ranger patch. Too young to qualify? The park also has a Little Cub booklet that lets kids ages three to six qualify for an official button.

Nearby and a short step up in comfort from Curry Village, **Housekeeping Camp** has a wonderful location on a sandy beach along the Merced River with a view of Yosemite Falls. Each of the 226 units has a canvas roof and a concrete floor

Housekeeping Camp at Curry Village.

and three concrete walls. The fourth "wall" is a canvas curtain separating the sleeping area from the covered patio, enclosed by a wooden privacy fence. The sleeping area of each unit has a double bed and two fold-down bunks, as well as a table and chairs. Bed linens are not provided, but bedrolls can be rented for a small fee. The patio has a picnic table, a barbecue grill, and a bear box for food storage. There are electric lighting and outlets but no phones, televisions or indoor plumbing. All units share central restrooms and showers. ~ BUDGET.

Yosemite Lodge stands on the former site of Fort Yosemite, headquarters for the U.S. Army cavalrymen who served as park rangers in the days before the National Park Service was formed. The fort was torn down and the lodge was built in 1915 to accommodate the rapid growth of tourism in the park; it was refurbished and landscaped with local trees and plants to restore the buildings' harmony with their surroundings. Most of the 229 guest rooms are in long, low buildings that surround the central lodge. Each of these "lodge rooms" is spacious and has two double beds, a table and chairs, a private bath, a separate dressing area, a telephone and a patio or balcony. There are also 19 smaller "standard rooms" that have most of the

Fit for a Lady

The concept for the Ahwahnee Hotel came about in the early 1920s, when Yosemite was visited by Lady Astor, England's first female Member of Parliament and also the first American-born MP. She was scheduled to stay in the now-vanished Sentinel Hotel, but when she saw the rough-hewn, unheated lodge, she turned around and retreated in a huff to the more civilized surroundings of San Francisco, where she wrote a letter of complaint to President Woodrow Wilson. By way of response, the head of the National Park Service directed the Curry Company to build a hotel that would meet the high standards of European nobility. Among the Ahwahnee's guests since it opened its doors in 1927: three U.S. presidents and Queen Elizabeth II—as well as 350 U.S. Navy servicemen who stayed there while the grand hotel served as a rehabilitation center during World War II.

same features but no patios. None of the rooms have televisions. ~ DELUXE.

Of course, when money is no object, my favorite place to bed down in the valley is the **Ahwahnee Hotel**. From the moment you step into the lobby, with its massive granite hearths, sparkling chandeliers, beamed ceilings and American Indian artifacts, you know you're in a place that's unique even among world-class hotels. The Indian motif is carried into the 99 guest rooms in the main lodge, each of which boasts a magnificent view of Half Dome, Glacier Point or Yosemite Falls. Each room has either a king-size bed or two double beds and a full complement of quality furnishings including deep upholstered chairs. Housekeeping service includes evening turndown. A few rooms connect to parlors so that they can be converted into suites. The 24 cottage rooms, set amid manicured lawns and arbors of pine and dogwood, have decor and furnishings similar to the main lodge facilities. The Ahwahnee has the only rooms in the valley with TV sets. No air conditioning. ~ 559-252-4848, fax 559-456-0542. ULTRA-DELUXE.

A CAMP IS BORN

David and Jenny Curry started the Curry Camping Company (later renamed the Yosemite Park & Curry Company) in 1899 to provide modestly priced food and lodging for Yosemite visitors. Their motto was "A good bed and a clean napkin with every meal." **Curry Village** has operated continuously during the warm months ever since.

Reservations are essential during the summer at all Yosemite accommodations and year-round at Yosemite Lodge and the Ahwahnee Hotel. To secure a room at the Ahwahnee, reservations should be made six months or more in advance. Contact **Yosemite Reservations, Yosemite Concession Services**. ~ 5410 East Home Avenue, Fresno, CA 93727; 559-252-4848, fax 559-456-0542; www.yosemitepark.com.

dining

Yosemite Village has a cluster of eateries, all of which evolved from a bakery that Bridget Degnan, the wife of a park employee, started in her house in 1915. Today the complex includes **Degnan's Delicatessen**, which still serves baked goods as well as other

Eat, Drink and Be Merry

Throughout the winter months, the Ahwahnee Hotel is the scene of lavish feasts and celebrations. The season starts with an eight-week series of weekend **Vintners Holidays**, where each weekend industry experts and four different California wineries offer seminars, panel discussions and wine tastings, followed by an elegant five-course dinner each weekend from early November to early December. Christmas is celebrated with the **Bracebridge Dinner**, a tradition since 1927 in which more than 100 performers re-create a 17th-century English manor house feast complete with rituals, Olde English music and a seven-course dinner (make reservations up to a year ahead). The Ahwahnee rings out the old year with a black-tie **New Year's Eve Dinner Dance**, so popular that all reservations are awarded by lottery held the preceding February. Throughout January and early February, the Ahwahnee has two- and three-day **Chef's Holidays** twice a week, featuring cooking demonstrations by America's top chefs and a gala five-course dinner. All of these events are special packages that include lodging at the Ahwahnee or the less pricey Yosemite Lodge. ~ 559-252-4848.

delicacies that you can eat on the premises or pack away for a picnic lunch. ~ BUDGET. Adjoining the deli, **Degnan's Fast Food** serves fried chicken and fixin's year-round. ~ BUDGET. The **Village Grill** offers a burgers-and-fries menu. Closed in winter. ~ BUDGET TO MODERATE. There is also **Degnan's Ice Cream and Frozen Yogurt**. ~ BUDGET.

The Loft is located upstairs from the other Degnan enterprises. It offers the only sit-down dining option in Yosemite Village, with a buffet featuring pasta and kabobs and roast chicken as well as soup and salads. No lunch on weekdays. ~ MODERATE.

The **Curry Village Pavilion** offers all-you-can-eat breakfast and dinner buffets daily between Memorial Day and Labor Day. Curry Village also has several fast-food concessions, including the Taqueria Stand, the Pizza Patio, the Curry Coffee Corner and the Curry Ice Cream Stand. Open April through October. ~ Curry Village. BUDGET.

In Yosemite Lodge, the **Food Court** may bring back memories of your school cafeteria with its buffet line and vast, fluorescent-lit dining area. After a hard day's hike, the array of steaming entrées and tempting desserts may

OPPOSITE: The Ahwahnee Hotel.

The Ahwahnee Hotel's Great Lounge.

make ambience inconsequential—and the price is certainly right. ~ BUDGET.

Fine dining is available at Yosemite Lodge in the **Mountain Room**. The restaurant's interior, with its warm, modern ambience, is upstaged by the fact that nearly every table in the house enjoys a spectacular view of Yosemite Falls through floor-to-ceiling windows. The menu focuses on steak, seafood, chicken and pasta, and the cuisine is far from routine. Dinner only. ~ 209-372-1274. DELUXE.

Among Yosemite Valley restaurants, the pièce de résistance is the elegant **Ahwahnee Dining Room**. The restaurant occupies one whole wing of the hotel, and like the lobby it features stone, glass and high beamed ceilings along with American Indian decorative elements. The service is impeccable, as you might expect from the only restaurant in the park with a dress code at dinner. The menu is as tantalizing as it is pricey. Breakfast options include peppered filet mignon and eggs and a smoked fish sampler of trout, salmon and ahi tuna. Dinner might be pan-roasted duck breast with black truffle potatoes or, for vegetarians, wild mushroom risotto cannoli. ~ 209-372-1489. ULTRA-DELUXE.

Although most nightlife in Yosemite is of the four-legged variety, if you wish you can celebrate the conclusion of an adventure-packed day with cocktails at Yosemite Lodge's **Mountain Room Bar** or the Ahwahnee Hotel's atmospheric **Indian Room Bar**. Both bars have big fireplaces that roar and crackle during the cold months. For family fun after dark, try **Yosemite Theater Live**, presented at the East Auditorium behind the Visitors Center most nights. Recent shows have included a live one-man show portraying John Muir. The shows often sell out, so buy tickets in advance at any tour desk in the park.

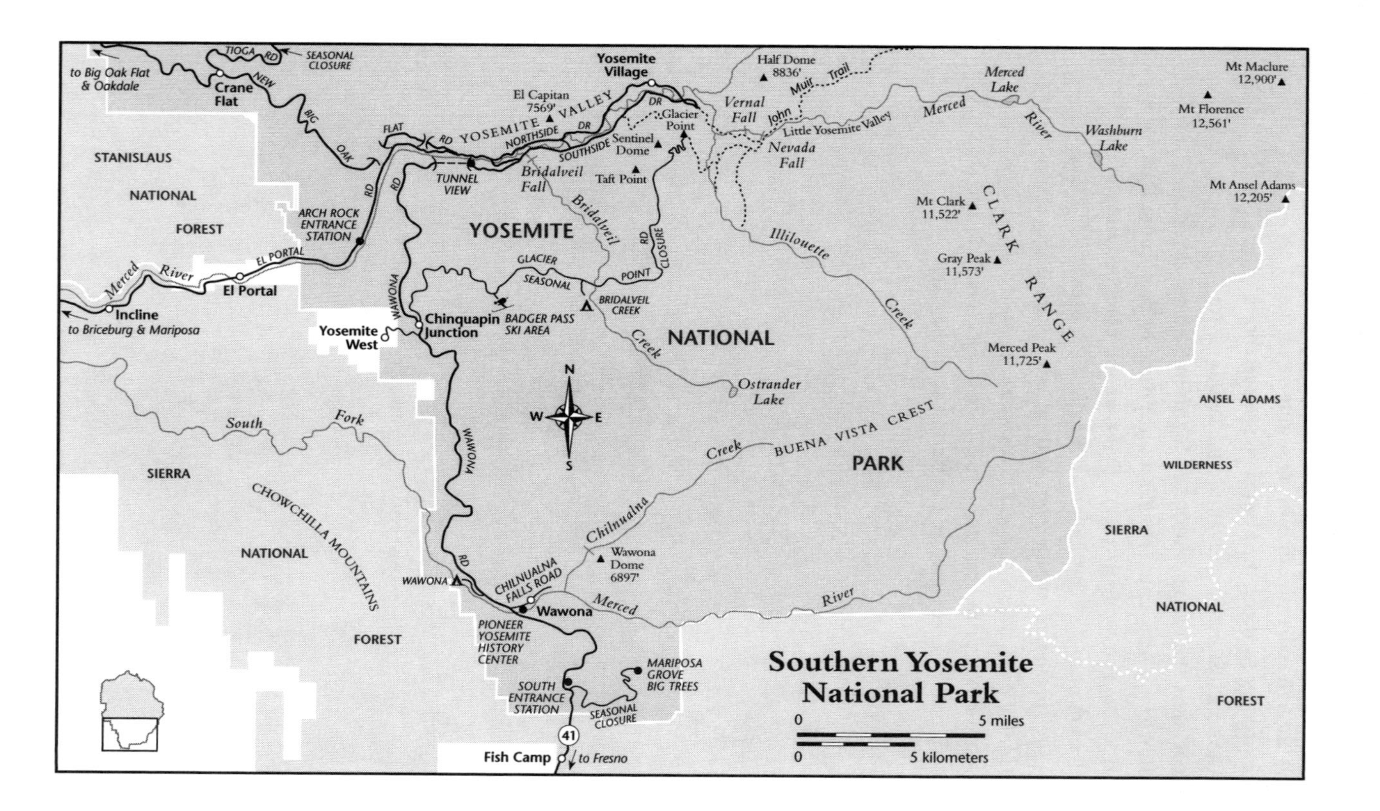
Southern Yosemite National Park
0 5 miles
0 5 kilometers
to Big Oak Flat & Oakdale
TIOGA RD
SEASONAL CLOSURE
Crane Flat
NEW BIG OAK FLAT RD
Yosemite Village
El Capitan 7569'
YOSEMITE VALLEY
NORTHSIDE DR
SOUTHSIDE DR
Half Dome 8836'
John Muir Trail
Vernal Fall
Nevada Fall
Little Yosemite Valley
Glacier Point
Sentinel Dome
Taft Point
Merced Lake
Merced River
Washburn Lake
Mt Maclure 12,900'
Mt Florence 12,561'
Mt Ansel Adams 12,205'
STANISLAUS NATIONAL FOREST
TUNNEL VIEW
Bridalveil Fall
Bridalveil Creek
ARCH ROCK ENTRANCE STATION
EL PORTAL RD
Merced River
El Portal
Incline
to Briceburg & Mariposa
YOSEMITE NATIONAL PARK
GLACIER POINT RD SEASONAL CLOSURE
BRIDALVEIL CREEK
BADGER PASS SKI AREA
Chinquapin Junction
WAWONA RD
Yosemite West
Illilouette Creek
Mt Clark 11,522'
Gray Peak 11,573'
CLARK RANGE
Merced Peak 11,725'
Ostrander Lake
BUENA VISTA CREST
Chilnualna Creek
N
W
E
S
South Fork
SIERRA NATIONAL FOREST
CHOWCHILLA MOUNTAINS
Wawona Dome 6897'
CHILNUALNA FALLS ROAD
WAWONA
Wawona
Merced River
PIONEER YOSEMITE HISTORY CENTER
MARIPOSA GROVE BIG TREES
SOUTH ENTRANCE STATION
SEASONAL CLOSURE
41
Fish Camp
to Fresno
ANSEL ADAMS WILDERNESS
SIERRA NATIONAL FOREST

3

Southern Yosemite National Park

How John Muir's words moved the U.S. Congress to create Yosemite National Park in 1890 is a tale so familiar that it has become perhaps the first true legend of the American environmental movement. Fewer people realize, however, that Yosemite had been declared a California state park decades earlier, five years before Muir set foot in the area for the first time.

It was a much smaller park then, divided into two separate units that were several days' horseback ride apart. One unit, of course, was Yosemite Valley. The other was the area now known as Wawona, site of the Mariposa Grove of sequoias, a sight as astonishing to visitors today as it was in 1857, when mountain man

Galen Clark first explored the grove and started building a tourist hotel nearby.

As Yosemite was expanded into the national park we know today, most of its 760,000-acre expanse was preserved as roadless wilderness, accessible only by more than 800 miles of hiking and horse trails. All of it is now permanently protected under the federal Wilderness Act of 1964. To get a hint of what this really means, take the scenic drives through the southern part of the park to Glacier Point and Wawona. Although it takes an hour to drive from Yosemite Valley to either destination, the roads only skirt the edge of a vast, primeval landscape. An eagle could soar eastward over the jagged granite crags of the Clark Range and beyond to the equally high peaks of the Cathedral Range, farther than a hiker could trek in a week, and never fly over a road or beyond the national park boundary. Fortunately for visitors, some of the park's most dramatic sights are far easier to reach.

OPPOSITE: View of Half Dome from Glacier Point.

sightseeing

As you drive out of Yosemite Valley, take a left at the first fork in the road, marked Route 41 to Glacier Point and Wawona. Near the fork in the road is the trailhead to an easy quarter-mile walk that takes you to the foot of **Bridalveil Fall**, a Yosemite landmark that plunges 620 feet from the brink of a cliff hidden in an alcove between Leaning Tower and Cathedral Spires. Flowing strong with spring runoff, the waterfall casts a spray that soaks onlookers; by fall, it subsides into silvery trickles weaving their way down the cliff.

Bridalveil Fall.

A parking lot for the Bridalveil Fall trail is located just before a tunnel on Route 41. Be sure to stop at the vista point called **Tunnel View** for a classic view of Yosemite Valley, with Half Dome perfectly framed between El Capitan and Cathedral Spires.

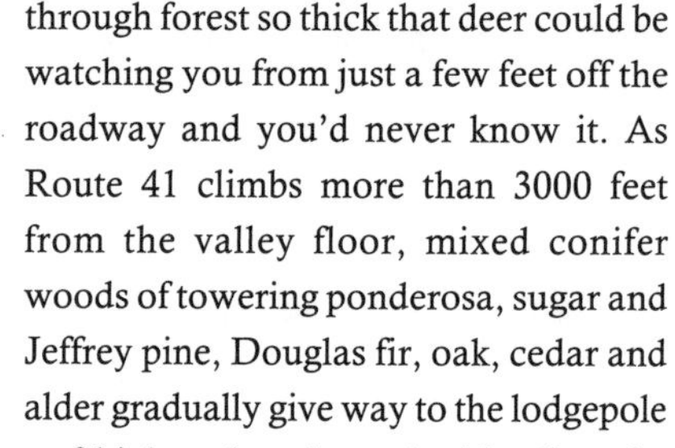

Beyond the tunnel, drive 15 miles through forest so thick that deer could be watching you from just a few feet off the roadway and you'd never know it. As Route 41 climbs more than 3000 feet from the valley floor, mixed conifer woods of towering ponderosa, sugar and Jeffrey pine, Douglas fir, oak, cedar and alder gradually give way to the lodgepole pine and red fir forest of higher elevations. At 15 miles, the road divides. Keep to the left, following the sign marked Glacier Point, and a few twisting miles will bring you to the **Badger Pass Ski Area**. Beyond this point, Glacier Point Road is closed in winter.

Glacier Point Road ends in a large though not always adequate parking lot, from which a paved footpath leads downhill to **Glacier Point** and one of the most impressive views in the park. From a vantage of 7214 feet directly above Curry Village, you can peer down on Yosemite Village and Yosemite

Badger Pass Ski Area.

Falls. Turn your gaze northward for a panoramic view of the Yosemite wilderness, with its boundless forest and walls of high peaks frosted with snow even in midsummer.

If you stay on Route 41 instead of turning off on Glacier Point Road, another 15-mile drive through the forest will bring you to **Wawona**, just inside the south entrance to Yosemite. Because some 19th-century buildings, including the stately old Wawona Hotel, still stand here, park rangers have dubbed this the historic section of the park. Here, the **Pioneer Yosemite History Center** showcases pioneer cabins, a blacksmith shop, a Wells Fargo office and a cavalry office that served as the national park headquarters at the beginning of the 1900s. I like to wander among the old cabins and residences, including the original Degnan's Bakery from Yosemite Village, that have been moved here from elsewhere in the park. There's also a collection of wagons and buckboards. A covered bridge

JUST FOR KIDS: STAGECOACH RIDES

Wawona was the main stagecoach stop for Yosemite in the late 19th century. The people who operated the stage company also owned the Wawona Hotel, so every stagecoach passenger spent the night there before making the all-day trip to Yosemite Valley. The stages—actually open-air carriages with removable canvas roofs for bad weather—are still used to carry kids and families on rides around the Pioneer Yosemite History Center in the summertime.

Little-known Sequoia Facts

- The first report about the existence of sequoias was to be published by a Pennsylvania newspaper in 1839. But the newspaper never reached readers because the printing company burned down, so sequoias were not "officially" discovered until 13 years later.
- A cross-section of a sequoia trunk was shipped to the U.S. Centennial Exposition in 1876—but it was denounced as a fraud because timber experts asserted that no tree could grow that large.
- Although a mature sequoia can weigh as much as two million pounds, its seeds are so small that it takes 91,000 of them to weigh just one pound.
- There is no theoretical limit to the size of a sequoia, since it continues to grow throughout its life and never dies of old age. But for lightning strikes and cutting by humans, the giant trees would be virtually immortal.

over the creek that flows past the center replicates the one that used to carry all visitors into the park; the original was destroyed by a flood in 1955.

Of the three groves of sequoia trees in Yosemite National Park, the largest is **Mariposa Grove Big Trees**, where about 200 trees measure more than ten feet in diameter. The trees, which can weigh more than 2,000,000 pounds, are the largest living organisms on earth, and some are among the oldest, such as the grove's Grizzly Giant, which has been determined by tree-ring dating to be more than 2700 years old. Long, train-like trams run every 20 minutes, so for most of the day the grove is filled with sightseers. Yet one of the more striking phenomena you may observe in the grove is the cathedral silence that prevails as hundreds of sightseers are struck dumb by the sequoias' majesty.

outdoor adventures

HIKING

Several of the most spectacular hikes (distances listed for all hiking trails are one way unless otherwise noted) in Yosemite National Park start from Glacier Point. Among the easy ones is the 1.1-mile **Sentinel Dome Trail**, which climbs a mere 370 feet from the parking lot trailhead to the summit of a dome overlooking Yosemite Valley directly across from Yosemite Falls. Unlike Glacier Point, the top of Sentinel Dome offers an unobstructed 360-degree view that takes in nearly the entire park.

Another scenic short hike from Glacier Point, the 1.1-mile **Taft Point Trail** descends slightly to pass The Fissures, a series of crevices through which you can look straight down into Yosemite Valley, on its way to Taft Point. The exposed, overhanging point overlooks the part of the valley between Yosemite Falls and El Capitan, and was named for the U.S. President who visited the park in 1909. Though an easy hike, this is not a trail to take with young children; the edgy point has rough footing and no guard rail.

Sequoia trees at Wawona.

For a more challenging hike from Glacier Point, try the **Panorama Trail** from the northeast side of the parking area. The trail goes 2.1 miles, descending 1400 feet on its way to 370-foot Illilouette Fall. The trail descends by switchbacks through a recovering forest fire area, then continues into the impressive Illilouette Gorge, which slices its way through the Panorama Cliffs. Though the climb back up to Glacier Point might seem daunting, it's no worse than the climb you would face up the other side of the gorge if you decided to continue on the trail, passing Nevada and Vernal falls on your way down to the Yosemite Valley floor.

Hikers who ride the shuttle up to Glacier Point can return to Yosemite Valley via **Four Mile Trail**, which descends more than 3000 feet—much of it by switchbacks and steeply sloping ridgelines—to come out at Southside Drive near the base of Sentinel Rock. Actually 4.6 miles one-way, the trail can be hiked downhill in about two hours, and the gorgeous scenery is nonstop.

Near Wawona, several walking trails meander among the giant sequoias of **Mariposa Grove**. Free shuttle buses carry sightseers through the grove, but you can appreciate the setting far more by walking around the labyrinth of paths that intersect to form loop routes varying from 1.6 miles to 6 miles or more. The best places to start are the parking lot at the south end of the grove or any of the more famous "big trees," including Fallen Monarch, the Grizzly Giant and the California Tunnel Tree.

It is also possible to hike from the **Wawona Hotel to Mariposa Grove**, a strenuous 16-mile partial loop that starts by following the bridle trail from the Wawona Stables. The hiking trail leaves the horse trail after two miles, passing through forested bowls and eventually climbing by switchbacks to a high ridge, then descending to join the maze of footpaths through the sequoia grove.

SKIING

The only downhill skiing in Yosemite is at **Badger Pass Ski Area**, the oldest ski area in California. Except for the addition of five chairlifts, the ski area still appears much as it did when the Yosemite Winter Club built it in 1935. There are ten runs, rated 35 percent beginner, 50 percent intermediate and 15 percent advanced, with a vertical drop of 800 feet; snowboarding is allowed. Visitors staying in Yosemite Valley can get special discount-priced packages that include free shuttle to the ski area, a lift ticket, two lessons and babysitting services. Ski rentals are available. Open mid-December to early April. ~ Glacier Point Road; 209-372-8430, snow conditions 209-372-1000; www.yosemitepark.com.

Located at the Badger Pass Ski Lodge, the **Yosemite Cross Country**

HOME IN THE SNOW

The ultimate cross-country ski experience in Yosemite, the overnight trip up Bridalveil Creek to Ostrander Lake takes you 2.5 miles from Badger Pass Ski Area, paralleling the closed-in-winter Glacier Point Road, to Bridalveil Creek Campground, then 6.7 more miles up the creek to the lake. The trip takes at least six hours each way in good weather. Fortunately, there's a place to stay by the lake. The dormitory-style Ostrander Ski Hut, which sleeps 25, has become so popular—especially on weekends—that reservations are only available by a lottery held in November for the coming ski season. To enter the lottery, contact the Ostrander Hut Wilderness Office. ~ 209-372-0740.

Ski Center offers classes ranging from beginners' courses to advanced telemarking lessons, as well as guided tours to Glacier Point or other backcountry destinations. Visitors can also rent "skinny-skis" and explore some 75 miles of trails groomed or at least broken for cross-country skiing. ~ 209-372-8344; www.yosemitepark.com.

GOLF

Whatever the **Wawona Golf Course** may lack as a challenging course is more than compensated for by the fresh mountain air and beautiful pine forest setting adjacent to the Wawona Hotel. The nine-hole, par-35 golf course is relatively short—only 3035 yards. When it opened in 1918, it was the first golf course in the Sierra Nevada. Today it has a pro shop where carts and clubs are available for rent. ~ 209-375-6556.

HORSEBACK RIDING

Two-hour guided horseback rides along a forested ridge above the Wawona Hotel are offered daily from May through October at **Wawona Stables** near the Pioneer Yosemite History Center. Check with the stables or at the hotel desk for longer half-day and all-day trips that are offered intermittently through the week. Reservations are essential. ~ 209-375-6502.

CAMPING

Bridalveil Creek Campground is set at a chilly 7200-foot elevation, midway up Glacier Point Road. Surrounded by forest at a distance from the main road, it seems to be in a different world from busy Yosemite Valley, just a few miles away as the crow flies and 3000 feet straight down. There are 110 tent/RV sites, $12 per night, first-come, first-served. Facilities include restrooms and drinking water, but no hookups. A horse corral is provided for groups planning pack trips into the wilderness. Open July to early September. ~ Glacier Point Road, Mile 25.

Wawona Campground has 93 tent/RV sites. The elevation of 4000 feet makes for year-round camping. This is the only campground in the park that's close enough to Mariposa Grove to let you stroll among the ancient sequoias in the early morning mist, before the crowds arrive. There are restrooms and drinking water, but no hookups; a grocery store and riding stable are nearby. Sites cost $18 per night May through September, $12 October through April. Reservations are required May through September; first-come, first-served the rest of the year. ~ Located on a side road 1.5 miles inside the Wawona entrance to the park (Route 41 from Fresno); 800-436-7275; reservations.nps.gov.

OVER THE EDGE

One look over the brink at Glacier Point is enough to convince most people that leaping off with only a hang glider to protect you from splattering the pavement 3000 feet down would be tantamount to suicide. But in fact, there are those who do it and live to tell the tale. There's even a **Yosemite Hang Gliding Association**. To do it yourself, you need a Hang IV certification, and the association must agree to sponsor you. Good luck. ~ 719-632-8300.

Merced Recreation Area, in the Sierra foothills seven to ten miles outside the park boundary, offers a great alternative for visitors who are too spontaneous to make campground reservations months in advance or who just want to camp at a distance from the Yosemite Valley crowds. Set along an idyllic stretch of the Merced River, the recreation area's three campgrounds—**McCabe Flat**, **Willow Placer** and **Railroad Flat**—offer a combined total of 21 walk-in tent sites and 9 sites suitable for tents or small RVs (up to 18 feet). The river offers good flyfishing, and a former railroad grade beyond the last campground makes for good hiking or mountain biking. There are vault toilets but no drinking water or hookups. Sites cost $10 per night, first-come, first-served. Open year-round. ~ To get there, take Route 140 from Yosemite's Arch Rock entrance west (toward Merced) to Briceburg. Turn right at the Bureau of Land Management's Briceburg Visitors Center on the road marked "BLM Camping Areas." The campgrounds are 2.5, 3.8 and 4.8 miles down this road; 916-985-4474.

lodging

Besides the landmark Wawona Hotel, the other lodging in this part of the park is at **The Redwoods in Yosemite**—actually a collection of 130 privately owned and individually furnished vacation homes and cabins, which the owners rent out to park visitors when not staying there themselves. Secluded in shady pine forest, they range from compact one-bedroom cabins to six-bedroom houses. All but the smallest have fireplaces or woodburning stoves. Other amenities include fully equipped kitchenettes or kitchens, telephones and televisions with VCRs. Some have dishwashers, decks with barbecues and hot tubs. Daily maid service is available for an additional charge. ~ Box 2085, Wawona Station; 209-375-6666, fax 209-375-6400; www.redwoodsinyosemite.com, e-mail info@redwoodsinyosemite.com. MODERATE TO ULTRA-DELUXE.

Sleeping with the Past

The oldest surviving hotel in Yosemite National Park, the stately white **Wawona Hotel** presides over its broad, neatly manicured lawn with the air of a gracious antebellum Southern mansion. The 104 guest rooms are in the main hotel building

(dating back to 1879) and in five other buildings that also feature the hotel's trademark verandas. The rooms are cozy and individually furnished, often with brass beds or rustic antiques. Only 50 rooms have private baths; the rest share central restrooms and showers down the hall. The hotel has a small swimming pool and a tennis court. ~ 209-375-6556, fax 209-375-6601. MODERATE TO DELUXE.

The Tenaya Lodge at Yosemite.

Or venture outside the national park boundary to the little village of Fish Camp, where the **Tenaya Lodge at Yosemite** offers 244 rooms and suites. Rustic in feel, each room is comfortably appointed in earth-tone fabrics and wood trim with artwork and warm lighting. Built in 1990, the hotel is set amid landscaped grounds bordering 35 acres of Sierra National Forest, and has outdoor swimming pools, jacuzzis, a gym and a cocktail lounge. If that isn't enough luxury, room amenities include telephones, coffeemakers and cable television with movies and Nintendo to order. ~ 1122 Route 41, Fish Camp; 559-683-6555, 888-514-2167, fax 559-683-6147; www.tenayalodge.com, e-mail jfarrington@destinationtravel.com. ULTRA-DELUXE.

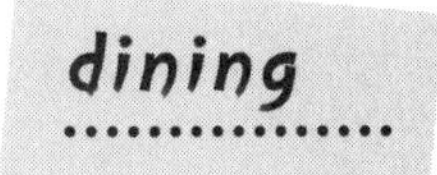

The **Wawona Hotel Dining Room** offers a steadily changing menu of fine-dining selections such as prime rib, filet mignon and rainbow trout in an elegant atmosphere defined by turn-of-the-20th-century decor and panoramic views. The restaurant operates daily from Easter week through October, on Thanksgiving Day and through Christmas week; the rest of the year it's open Friday through Sunday only, closed the first two weeks of December. Although there is no explicit dress code, guests are asked to wear "tasteful, casual clothing" befitting the dignified atmosphere of the restaurant. The Wawona Hotel also hosts a traditional **pit barbecue** on Saturdays during the summer, serving steaks, hamburgers and corn-on-the-cob outdoors on red checkered tablecloths. ~ 209-375-6556, fax 209-375-6601. MODERATE TO DELUXE.

In the Tenaya Lodge at Yosemite, the **Sierra Room** is a contemporary restaurant with a lofty skylight ceiling and a towering limestone fireplace. The fare, characterized as "Sierra cuisine," features fresh produce and entrées such as cedar-plank roasted salmon, Sacramento Delta paella and San Joaquin Valley rabbit braised in zinfandel. The lodge also offers more casual dining experiences at its coffee shop and deli. ~ 1122 Route 41, Fish Camp; 559-683-6555. MODERATE TO DELUXE.

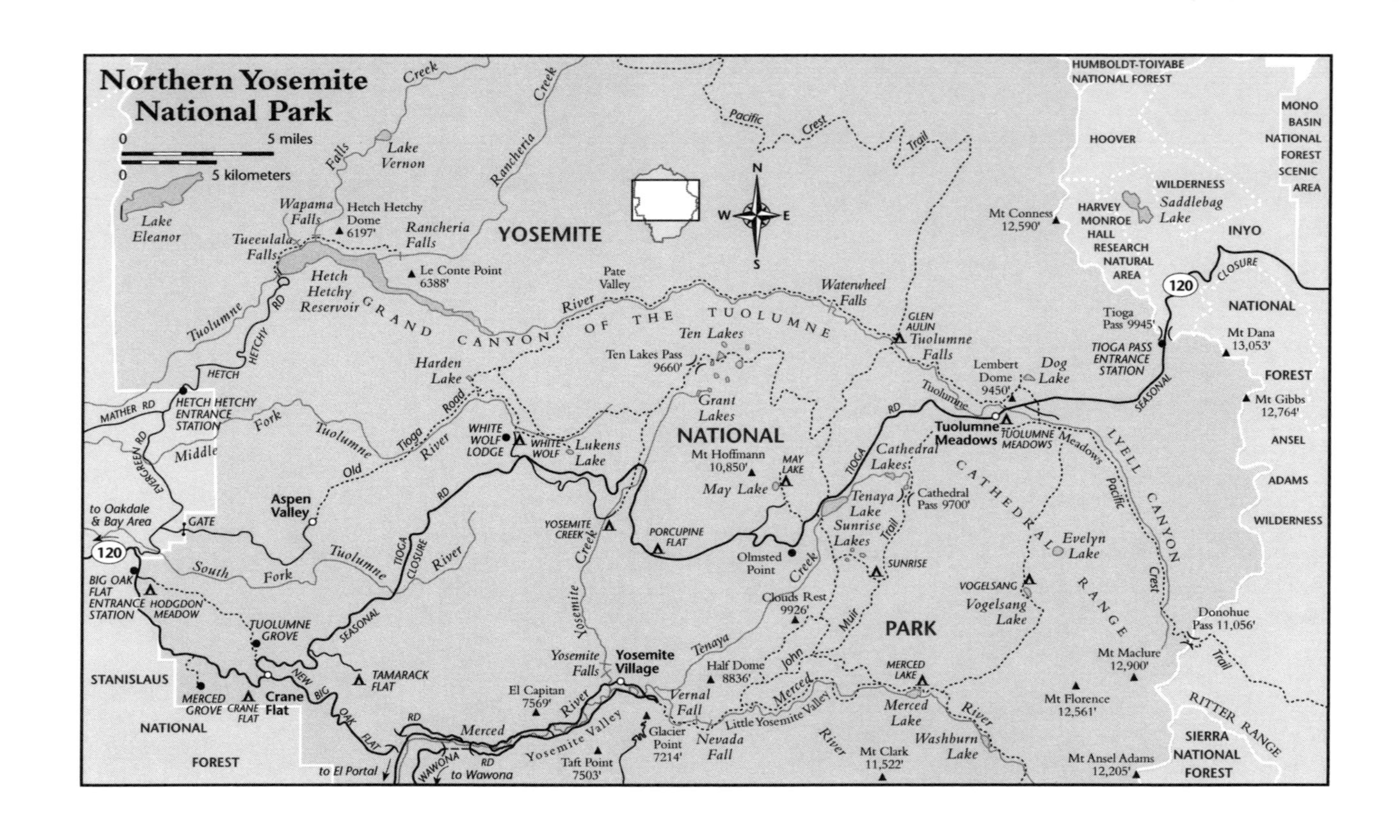

Northern Yosemite National Park
0 5 miles
0 5 kilometers
YOSEMITE
NATIONAL
PARK
Lake Eleanor
Lake Vernon
Falls
Creek
Rancheria Creek
Wapama Falls
Hetch Hetchy Dome 6197'
Rancheria Falls
Tueeulala Falls
Hetch Hetchy Reservoir
Le Conte Point 6388'
GRAND CANYON OF THE TUOLUMNE
Pate Valley
River
Waterwheel Falls
GLEN AULIN
Tuolumne Falls
Pacific Crest Trail
Ten Lakes
Ten Lakes Pass 9660'
Harden Lake
Grant Lakes
Mt Hoffmann 10,850'
MAY LAKE
May Lake
Tuolumne
HETCH HETCHY RD
HETCH HETCHY ENTRANCE STATION
MATHER RD
EVERGREEN RD
Middle Fork Tuolumne
Tioga Road
Old
River
WHITE WOLF LODGE
WHITE WOLF
Lukens Lake
Aspen Valley
to Oakdale & Bay Area
GATE
120
South Fork Tuolumne River
TIOGA RD
SEASONAL CLOSURE
BIG OAK FLAT ENTRANCE STATION
HODGDON MEADOW
TUOLUMNE GROVE
STANISLAUS NATIONAL FOREST
MERCED GROVE
CRANE FLAT
Crane Flat
NEW BIG OAK FLAT RD
TAMARACK FLAT
to El Portal
WAWONA RD
to Wawona
YOSEMITE CREEK
Yosemite Creek
PORCUPINE FLAT
Olmsted Point
Yosemite Falls
Yosemite Village
El Capitan 7569'
Merced River
Yosemite Valley
Taft Point 7503'
Glacier Point 7214'
Vernal Fall
Nevada Fall
Half Dome 8836'
Clouds Rest 9926'
Tenaya Creek
John Muir Trail
Little Yosemite Valley
Merced
River
Mt Clark 11,522'
MERCED LAKE
Merced Lake
Washburn Lake
Tenaya Lake
Sunrise Lakes
Trail
SUNRISE
Cathedral Lakes
Cathedral Pass 9700'
CATHEDRAL RANGE
Evelyn Lake
VOGELSANG
Vogelsang Lake
Tuolumne Meadows
TUOLUMNE MEADOWS
Lembert Dome 9450'
Dog Lake
Meadows
Pacific Crest
LYELL CANYON
Donohue Pass 11,056'
Trail
Mt Maclure 12,900'
Mt Florence 12,561'
Mt Ansel Adams 12,205'
RITTER RANGE
SIERRA NATIONAL FOREST
Mt Conness 12,590'
HUMBOLDT-TOIYABE NATIONAL FOREST
HOOVER WILDERNESS
HARVEY MONROE HALL RESEARCH NATURAL AREA
Saddlebag Lake
MONO BASIN NATIONAL FOREST SCENIC AREA
INYO NATIONAL FOREST
Tioga Pass 9945'
TIOGA PASS ENTRANCE STATION
SEASONAL CLOSURE
Mt Dana 13,053'
Mt Gibbs 12,764'
ANSEL ADAMS WILDERNESS
N
S
E
W

4

Northern Yosemite National Park

The other side of Yosemite National Park offers an experience quite different from that found in Yosemite Valley or Wawona. Lodging and other developed facilities are few and small, with the exception of the park's largest campground, as this area is geared more toward use by adventurers than casual sightseers. Once you've seen the High Sierra through your windshield, you're likely to experience an overwhelming temptation to get out and explore the mountain meadows and fantastic rock formations. The high country to the north and east of the park is ideal for hiking and horse or llama pack trips. This is not to suggest, however, that the Yosemite high country lacks interest for car tourists: Tioga Road, the single road across to the park's east

entrance, is a spectacular two-hour drive each way from Yosemite Village.

It was the High Sierra around Tuolumne Meadows that originally brought John Muir to Yosemite in 1868 as a young adventurer spending the summer among Basque shepherds. And 20 years later, it was the same High Sierra that led Muir to promote the idea of making Yosemite a national park. The main tourist areas, Yosemite Valley and Wawona, were already protected as a California state park. But Muir conceived the concept, strange even to most naturalists of his time, that the valley and the high mountains from which its waters came formed a single unified ecosystem. Unless the high country was also granted park protection, Muir feared, it would fall prey to overgrazing and ranch development that would eventually spell the end of Yosemite as he knew it. Today the area is off-limits to sheep grazing; instead it's a playground for many thousands of recreational users heading into the wilderness to retrace the paths Muir used to explore the park.

OPPOSITE: Tuolumne River.

During the winter months, Tioga Road and the Tioga Pass entrance to the park are closed, and all areas covered in this chapter, except Hetch Hetchy Reservoir and Tuolumne Grove, are inaccessible.

sightseeing

To reach the high country in the northwestern part of the park from Yosemite Valley, bear right each time the road divides. This will bring you to Crane Flat, where the only gas station in the main part of the park is located. Here you'll join Route 120 eastbound, also called Tioga Road. In a little over a mile, you'll pass the private, nonprofit **Yosemite Institute**, which presents week-long, hands-on environmental programs. The institute marks the start of the trail to the Tuolumne Grove sequoias (see "Hiking," later in this chapter). ~ Yosemite National Institute, P.O. Box 487, Yosemite, CA 95389; 209-379-9511, fax 209-379-9510; www.yni.org, e-mail yi@yni.org.

After several miles of winding through mixed conifer forest, Tioga Road crosses the South Fork of the Tuolumne River and begins a long, sustained ascent, traversing the slope of a long, wooded ridge, to an elevation of 8000 feet. You'll pass a turnoff on the left to **White Wolf**, a small lodge and camping area. Up to here, the road has proceeded without a single trailhead or parking area for more than ten miles; now you'll encounter about a dozen trailheads during the next half-hour of the drive. At the same time, the landscape broadens into expansive vistas of the

A PARK IS BORN

Just east of the Tuolumne Meadows visitors center, a short path across the meadows leads to the enclosed **Soda Springs**—fizzy but not good for drinking or swimming—and **Parsons Lodge**, an old overnight stop built by the Sierra Club in 1915 that now contains exhibits on the natural history of Yosemite's alpine meadows. The lodge marks the spot where, according to legend, John Muir first conceived the idea of creating Yosemite National Park.

A Kind of Immortality

Olmsted Point was named after one of America's greatest 19th-century architects, Frederick Law Olmsted, who is best known for designing Central Park in New York City. He was so impressed with Yosemite's beauty during an 1863 visit that he enlisted the support of California Senator John Conness to persuade the U.S. Congress and President Lincoln to deed the Yosemite Valley and Mariposa Grove to California as a state park. Mount Conness, one of the tallest peaks in today's Yosemite National Park, was named after the senator, and Mount Clark and the entire Clark Range were named after Galen Clark, the first superintendent of the new park. Curiously, no natural formation in Yosemite is named for the other person who was instrumental in turning it into a park—Abraham Lincoln.

distant Clark Range, with its cluster of skyscraping peaks—11,522-foot Mount Clark, 11,573-foot Gray Peak and 11,726-foot Merced Peak—grouped together in inaccessible grandeur.

At last the road comes to **Olmsted Point**, where you'll find a sizeable parking area—and no wonder: The point offers one of the most magnificent views in the entire park. Visitors who scramble to the top of the squat, fractured granite dome are rewarded with a view to the southwest straight down Little Yosemite Valley to the north side of Half Dome. In the opposite direction, **Tenaya Lake** gleams long and narrow along the side of Tioga Road as it continues to climb through the alpine terrain. More granite domes, many of them so crazed with fractures that gnarled whitebark pine trees anchor their roots on the rock faces, rise on both sides of the road as 12,590-foot **Mount Conness**

Lembert Dome.

The Smallest Big Tree Grove

Besides the park's two well-known sequoia groves, Tuolumne Grove and Mariposa Grove (see Chapter 3), there is a third, less-known grove in the park. Experts believe **Merced Grove** was part of Tuolumne Grove thousands of years ago when the climate was wetter than it is today. While there are fewer ancient giants here than in the other groves, there are more "young" sequoias, a mere 500 to 800 years old and five to eight feet in diameter. Although it is only a short distance off the main highway, Merced Grove receives fewer visitors because it is Yosemite's smallest sequoia grove and parking is extremely limited. Don't expect crowds or tourist shuttles. A 1.5-mile (one-way) trail starts near the Crane Flat road junction and leads to an old cabin at the far end of the grove.

comes into view in the distance, standing along the eastern park boundary.

Tuolumne Meadows is the hub of activity in the high country of Yosemite. The John Muir Trail and the Pacific Crest Trail join together in these gently rolling fields of mountain grasses and perennial herbs, patched with snow in spring, spangled with flowers in midsummer and golden in autumn, floating in a sea of lodgepole pine, red fir and hemlock. Pale rock domes, ghostly fossils of a mountain range that rose and subsided before the time of the dinosaurs, break through the soft surface. Foremost among them is 9450-foot **Lembert Dome**, a lopsided peak whose cold stone surface still gleams from the glacier that scoured and polished it during the Ice Ages.

At Tuolumne Meadows, during the summer months, you'll find a visitors center, a wilderness center, camping, food service and a gas station. Past the meadows, 13,053-foot **Mount Dana** and 12,764-foot **Mount Gibbs**, linked by a rock ridge, mark the park's eastern boundary. Midway between these mountains and Mount Conness to the north, a break in the wall of towering peaks allows the road to pass between them at an altitude of 9945 feet at Tioga Pass, the eastern park entrance and the highest mountain pass in California. Beyond that, the road suddenly plunges into the desert a mile below.

outdoor adventures

HIKING

The following is just a sample of the many hiking possibilities in the Tioga Road and Tuolumne Meadows area (all distances are one way unless otherwise noted).

Just after you turn onto Tioga Road, you'll have a chance to take a lovely walk through **Tuolumne Grove**, one of the three sequoia groves in the park (and, incidentally, one of only 75 such groves on the planet). The one-mile loop trail is a segment of Old Big Oak Flat Road that has been bypassed by present-day Route 120 and closed to vehicles. It descends 480 feet through a forest of fir, incense cedar and towering sugar pines before entering the grove of giant trees. A curiosity here is the Tunnel Tree, a lightning-struck sequoia stump through which someone cut a tunnel for the Old Big Oak Flat Road.

A sequoia dwarfs a visitor at Tuolumne Grove.

White Wolf, the lodge and camp midway up Tioga Road and a few miles off the main route, is the hub for a number of good hikes. It's 2.2 miles with a gradual descent to **Lukens Lake**, which is known for its exquisite summertime wildflower displays. Beyond the lake, the trail continues for another 1.5 miles to intersect Tioga Road, making it a good one-way walk for day-hikers who can arrange a car shuttle to drop them off at White Wolf and pick them up at the other end.

Another favorite day-hike from White Wolf, the **Harden Lake Trail** goes for three miles through virgin red fir forest to shallow Harden Lake, surrounded by rocks and gravel strewn by ancient glaciers. The lake is unusual in that it has no inlet or outlet; it grows during the spring as snow thaws from the surrounding slopes, then shrinks throughout the summer. As it becomes shallower, it also turns warm enough for swimming (but beware sharp rocks). The hike can be made into a loop trip by returning to White Wolf via the old Tioga Road, now closed to vehicles.

From Harden Lake, backpackers can follow the little-used trail westward down the South Fork of the Tuolumne River to **Aspen Valley**, a trip of 7.2 miles from the lake or about 10 miles from White Wolf. The trail was originally part of the old Tioga Road, and Aspen Valley was the original national park entrance until the 1940s.

Farther up Tioga Road, a trailhead on the north side of the road marks the start of the **Ten Lakes Trail**, a moderate two-day hike. It's a 5.5-mile trip from the main road, or a 7.6-mile trip from Yosemite Creek Campground, to the edge of the magnificent basin dotted with picture-perfect alpine lakes that reflect the high mountains surrounding them. Continuing to any

Mountain-high Hikes

The Tioga Road and Tuolumne Meadows area boasts an abundance of trailheads leading to more than 750 miles of trails within the national park as well as to the long-distance John Muir and Pacific Crest trails. Starting at elevations more than twice as high as the floor of Yosemite Valley, many of these trails make it easy to explore the alpine reaches of the High Sierra without requiring long, steep uphill climbs. Because of the thin air at these altitudes, however, visitors who live near sea level are advised to avoid long or strenuous hikes until their bodies have had a chance to acclimate (a minimum of several days).

of the lakes in the basin will add from one to three miles to the hike. Although this is one of the most popular destinations in the Tioga Road area, hikers find solitude as they disperse into various parts of the basin.

Between Olmsted Point and Tenaya Lake, the 2.7-mile trail that climbs north to **May Lake** is one of the most popular hikes in the high country. When you reach the lake, situated beneath the rock face of 10,850-foot Mount Hoffman, you'll see why: The beauty of the spot is breathtaking. There's a High Sierra Camp near the lake (reservations required), as well as restrooms and a small store that's open a few hours a day. Swimming and fishing are prohibited in the lake.

From the lower end of Tenaya Lake, the **Forsyth Trail** leads south toward Yosemite Valley, a one-way distance of 21.2 miles. At 2.5 miles, a side trail turns off to the east, passing Sunrise Lakes and continuing to join the John Muir Trail. Staying on the Forsyth Trail, you'll continue another 2.2 miles through the forest before reaching a fork in the trail. While both ways eventually lead to Little Yosemite Valley, the right-hand fork is the more scenic, climbing to the summit of **Clouds Rest** for one of the most spectacular views in the park before descending into the valley.

Perhaps the easiest hike in Tuolumne Meadows is the fascinating climb up **Pothole Dome**, a one-mile hike from a trailhead 1.5 miles west of the Tuolumne Meadows visitors center. The surface of the dome, polished smooth by glaciers, was pitted in ancient times by whirlpools of running water trapped beneath the glacial ice to form the "potholes" for which it is named.

From the main Tuolumne Meadows trailhead, the fairly easy **Dog Lake Loop Trail** (4.2 miles) skirts the sheer face of Lembert Dome on its way to an alpine lake partially surrounded by lodgepole pine forest at the edge of a meadow. Here you get a good view of Mount Dana and Mount Gibbs. The return trip takes you around the other side of the dome, crosses Tioga Road and winds up at the starting point.

Among the more ambitious hiking options at Tuolumne Meadows, the obvious choices are to take a segment of the **John Muir Trail** or the **Pacific Crest Trail**. The John Muir Trail runs more than 200 miles south to Mount Whitney, while the Pacific Crest Trail, the longest hiking trail in the United States, extends all the way from Mexico to Canada. You can hike the John Muir Trail southwest to Cathedral Lakes, a 4.6-mile dayhike starting at the Tuolumne Meadows Wilderness Center.

Yosemite's Lost Valley

John Muir called it "a wonderfully exact counterpart of the Merced Yosemite." State geologist Josiah Whitney remarked upon "how curiously nature has repeated itself" in the twin valleys. Yet no person alive today has seen the other valley both men were referring to—the Hetch Hetchy Valley on the Tuolumne River. While the Yosemite Valley was already a popular tourist destination, undeveloped Hetch Hetchy was an easy target for exploitation. In 1913, over the protests of Muir and the Sierra Club, the state of California authorized the damming and flooding of the valley to provide a reliable water supply for the city of San Francisco.

Today controversy rages over Hetch Hetchy once more as San Francisco seeks to expand the reservoir. Meanwhile, environmental groups demand that the present O'Shaughnessy Dam on the reservoir be demolished and the valley be allowed to revert to its natural state.

Although the reservoir itself is not open for recreational uses, visitors can drive to the dam and look downriver at what remains of the valley 2000 feet below. Hikers can also follow the 6.3-mile (one-way) **Rancheria Falls Trail** around the north side of the reservoir past Tueeulala and Wapama falls, then around 6197-foot Hetch Hetchy Dome to Rancheria Falls and Le Conte Point for a close-up view of the mouth of the Grand Canyon of the Tuolumne River. ~ To reach the dam and the trailhead, turn left on Evergreen Road just before the park boundary near the Big Oak Flat entrance on Route 120 West and drive 16 miles, passing through the park's Hetch Hetchy entrance station, to the parking area, where backpackers with wilderness permits can camp. The route to Hetch Hetchy Reservoir does not connect with any other park roads.

If you choose to follow the combined Pacific Crest and John Muir trails southeast from Tuolumne Meadows, a hike of about five miles will bring you to the upper end of **Lyell Canyon**, a broad, straight canyon 2000-feet deep with a chain of meadows along the canyon floor. This excursion is perhaps the most spectacular of the myriad one-day hiking options from Tuolumne Meadows. You can hike another ten miles before the trail climbs out of the canyon to leave the park via 11,056-foot Donohue Pass. Another long-distance trekking option is to make a grand loop trip by turning west at the trail junction midway down Lyell Canyon and hiking 6.3 miles past Evelyn Lake and over Tuolumne Pass to **Vogelsang**, where there is a High Sierra Camp (reservations required). From there, it's a 7.6-mile hike up Rafferty Creek to return to Tuolumne Meadows.

Perhaps the most irresistible hike from Tuolumne Meadows is to follow the Pacific Crest Trail northwest to **Glen Aulin**, a 5.7-mile hike across the meadows and past Tuolumne Falls. Although the roundtrip can easily be done as a day-hike, there is a High Sierra Camp (reservations required) at Glen Aulin. This is the starting point for the trail that branches off the Pacific Crest Trail to go down the **Grand Canyon of the Tuolumne River**, 14.3 challenging miles to the Pate Valley. The first leg of this spectacular trip follows the bottom of the canyon, then the trail climbs up to the north rim to navigate around the impassable Muir Gorge. There's backpacker camping near the Pate Valley river crossing. Rather than hike back up the canyon, you can cut at least a day off the roundtrip trek by continuing from the Pate Valley to Harden Lake, White Wolf Lodge and the Lukens Lake trailhead on Tioga Road, where you can catch the backpackers' shuttle. Allow three to four days for this trip.

CAMPING

Two campgrounds are located along Route 120 West (from Manteca) inside the Big Oak Flat entrance, the most used gateway to Yosemite National Park. The main virtue of **Hodgdon Meadow Campground**, with 110 sites just inside the park entrance, is that you can stake out your campsite first and have a home away from home to return to after exploring the park. There are restrooms and drinking water. The 4000-foot elevation makes for year-round camping. Sites cost $18 per night mid-April to mid-October, $12 mid-October to mid-April. Reservations required mid-April to mid-October; first-come, first-served the rest of the year. ~ Route 120 West; 800-436-7275; reservations.nps.gov.

The other Route 120 West camping area, **Crane Flat Campground**, is located ten miles inside the park entrance, just down the road from the main gas station, where a store sells groceries and camping supplies. The 166-site campground is also close to Tuolumne Grove. The 6200-foot elevation means that nighttime temperatures can run 20 degrees colder than at

Hot to Trot

Because of the long distances of some trails radiating from Tuolumne Meadows, this is a prime area for horseback and llama pack trips. Packers who bring their own stock can unload at the trailheads there; corrals are available, and the nearby national park stable provides overnight boarding services. Route and grazing restrictions apply, as well as limits on the number of people and animals in a group; a special stock permit is required. Inquire ahead of time by contacting the **Yosemite National Park Public Information Office**. ~ P.O. Box 577, Yosemite, CA 95389; 209-372-0200.

If you don't have a mount handy, some private outfitters are licensed to take horse and llama pack trips within the national park. For a listing of authorized commercial outfitters, contact **Eastern High Sierra Packers Association**. ~ 690 North Main Street, Bishop, CA 93514; 760-873-8405.

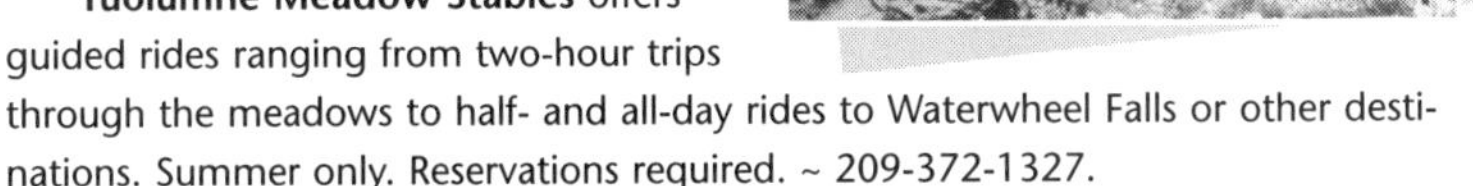

Tuolumne Meadow Stables offers guided rides ranging from two-hour trips through the meadows to half- and all-day rides to Waterwheel Falls or other destinations. Summer only. Reservations required. ~ 209-372-1327.

Multiday pack trips to the **High Sierra Camps** are also offered several times each summer. Reservations on these trips are only available by lottery; applications may be submitted between October 15 and November 30 of the preceding year. ~ 559-454-2002.

Hodgdon Meadow. Drinking water and restrooms are available. Sites cost $18 per night, reservations required. Open June through September. ~ Route 120 West; 800-436-7275; reservations.nps.gov.

A series of alpine campgrounds, each higher than the last, are found along Route 120 East (Tioga Road) as it makes its way among granite domes toward Tioga Pass and the high peaks that mark the park's eastern boundary. The turnoff to the first, **Tamarack Flat Campground**, is at 6300 feet, seven miles up Tioga Road from the Crane Flat junction. A rough side road, which turns off to the south and runs five miles to the campground, makes it inaccessible to trailers and large RVs. There are 52 tent sites, with outhouses but no drinking water (the park service says you can boil stream water for cooking and dishwashing). No pets. Sites cost $8 per night, first-come, first-served. Open June through September. ~ Route 120 East.

White Wolf Campground has 74 sites suitable for tents and small to midsize RVs (under 27 feet), with restrooms and drinking water but no hookups. You'll find a grocery store and food service nearby at White Wolf Lodge; rangers present evening campfire talks. At 8000 feet in elevation, the campground is the trailhead for day-hikes to Lukens Lake and Harden Lake and the east end of long treks to Ten Lakes or the Grand Canyon of the Tuolumne. Sites cost $12 per night, first-come, first-served. Open July to early September. ~ One mile off Route 120.

An unpaved, curvy, mildly hair-raising mountain road turns off Route 120 to the south shortly past the White Wolf junction and leads five miles to **Yosemite Creek Campground**. The road makes the campground inaccessible to trailers and

Backcountry Hosteling

The most unusual Yosemite lodging option is the five **High Sierra Camps** located at backcountry hiking destinations (Glen Aulin, May Lake, Sunrise Camp, Merced Lake and Vogelsang) 5.7 to 10 miles apart along a loop trail through the high country, ideal for week-long expeditions carrying minimal gear. Organized much like youth hostels, the camps offer dormitory-style accommodations in canvas tent cabins that sleep four or more hikers each on steel-frame beds with mattresses and blankets. Hikers must provide their own sheets or sleep-sacks and towels or make advance arrangements at the time of reservation to rent them. Restrooms are available; three of the five camps have hot showers, subject to water availability. Hearty, high-energy breakfasts and dinners (reservations required) are served in central dining tents, and box lunches are for sale. Sounds great—so what's the catch? The camps are so popular that the only way to get reservations is to enter a lottery. Applications are accepted October 15 through November 30 for the following summer; the lottery is held in mid-December. ~ To obtain a High Sierra Camp Lottery Application, call 559-454-2002. BUDGET.

large motorhomes (over 24 feet). At 7700 feet elevation, the 75 tent/RV sites have restrooms but no drinking water. (The park service says you can use stream water if you boil it first, and it may just be worth it so you can claim you drank from the same creek that tumbles over Yosemite Falls.) The hike downstream to the falls is the main reason for this campground's popularity. Sites cost $8 per night, first-come, first-served. Open July to early September. ~ Off Route 120.

Porcupine Flat Campground offers 52 sites, some but not all of them suitable for RVs. At 8100 feet elevation, this campground is about a mile from a trail junction where several hiking trails lead to points overlooking Yosemite Valley, about four miles straight-line distance to the south. There are outhouses but no drinking water (the campground is along a small stream whose water is said to be safe after boiling). No pets. Sites cost $8 per night, first-come, first-served. Open July through September. ~ Route 120.

The largest camping area in Yosemite National Park, with 304 sites as well as 25 walk-in sites for backpacker use and 7 group sites, **Tuolumne Meadows Campground** is also the highest in northern Yosemite (8600 feet) and the most distant from Yosemite Valley, two hours away by road. It's near the Tuolumne Meadows visitor center, where you can get a wilderness permit and rent a bear-resistant food canister. The main attractions are the John Muir Trail and the Pacific Crest Trail, which merge at the campground and continue southeast past the park boundary into the Ansel Adams Wilderness. Never mind the wide-open exposure the name suggests; the sites nestle among tall evergreens at the edge of the meadows. The camp-

ground has restrooms, drinking water and a dump station, but no hookups. Groceries, gasoline and horse stables are also nearby. Sites cost $18 per night. Half the sites are by reservation and the other half are first-come, first-served. Open June through September. ~ Route 120; 800-436-7275; reservations.nps.gov.

lodging

White Wolf Lodge has 24 canvas tent cabins with shared restrooms. Similar to those in Yosemite Valley's Curry Village, the wood-framed tents are set on raised wooden platforms and will sleep up to four people. They have beds with linens, candles, and wood-burning stoves, but no electricity. The lodge also has four wooden cabins with private baths, propane heating and limited electricity. Maid service is only provided in the private cabins with bath. Free shuttle service is available to Tenaya Lake and Tuolumne Meadows. Open mid-June to mid-September. ~ 209-372-1240. BUDGET TO MODERATE.

Set in a large meadow at an elevation of 8775 feet, **Tuolumne Meadows Lodge** rents 69 canvas tent cabins similar to those at Curry Village and White Wolf Lodge. They have beds with linens, candles, and woodburning stoves, but no electricity or maid service. Open mid-June to mid-September. ~ 209-372-1240. BUDGET.

dining

The indoor dining room in **White Wolf Lodge** serves breakfast and dinner daily during the summer months. Reservations are required for dinner. Guests at the lodge can also order box lunches at the front desk the night before. Open mid-June to mid-September. ~ 209-372-8416. MODERATE.

Tuolumne Meadows Lodge also serves a hearty family-style breakfast and dinner in its central dining tent. Dinner reservations are required. Guests can also order box lunches at the front desk the night before. Open mid-June to mid-September. ~ 209-372-8413. BUDGET.

The **Tuolumne Meadows Grill** serves burgers and other fast-food fare daily from Memorial Day weekend to late September, and limited groceries and picnic supplies are available at the **Tuolumne Meadows Store**, open in summer only. ~ BUDGET.

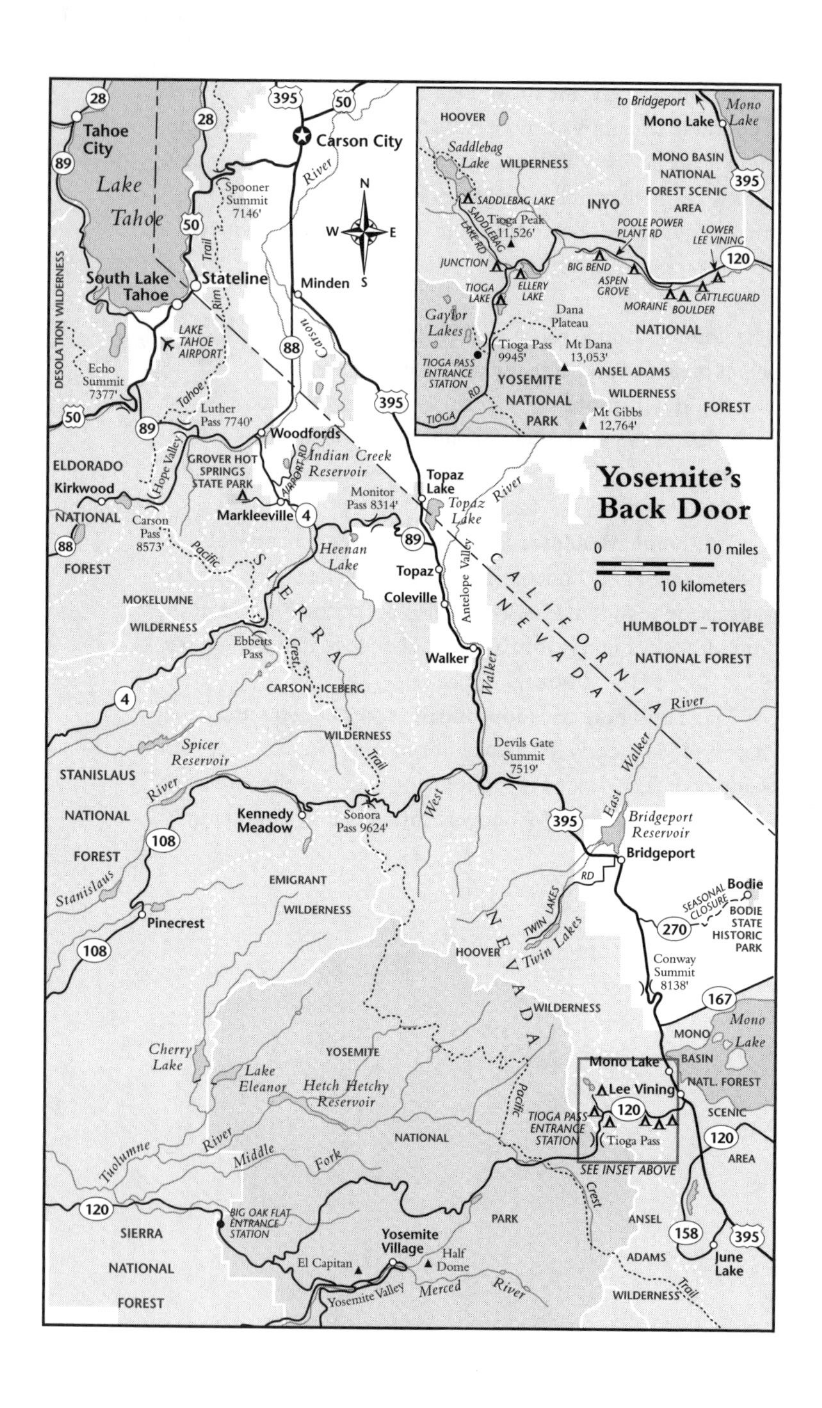
Yosemite's Back Door
0 10 miles
0 10 kilometers
Carson City
Tahoe City
Lake Tahoe
South Lake Tahoe
Stateline
Minden
Spooner Summit 7146'
Tahoe Rim Trail
LAKE TAHOE AIRPORT
Echo Summit 7377'
DESOLATION WILDERNESS
Luther Pass 7740'
Hope Valley
Woodfords
GROVER HOT SPRINGS STATE PARK
Indian Creek Reservoir
AIRPORT RD
ELDORADO
Kirkwood
NATIONAL
FOREST
Markleeville
Monitor Pass 8314'
Topaz Lake
Carson River
Carson Pass 8573'
Pacific Crest Trail
Heenan Lake
Topaz
Coleville
Antelope Valley
MOKELUMNE
WILDERNESS
Ebbetts Pass
SIERRA NEVADA
CALIFORNIA
NEVADA
Walker
Walker River
HUMBOLDT – TOIYABE
NATIONAL FOREST
CARSON ICEBERG
WILDERNESS
Spicer Reservoir
STANISLAUS
NATIONAL
FOREST
Stanislaus River
Devils Gate Summit 7519'
West Walker
East Walker River
Kennedy Meadow
Sonora Pass 9624'
Bridgeport Reservoir
Bridgeport
Bodie
SEASONAL CLOSURE
BODIE STATE HISTORIC PARK
EMIGRANT
WILDERNESS
Pinecrest
TWIN LAKES RD
Twin Lakes
HOOVER
WILDERNESS
Conway Summit 8138'
MONO BASIN NATL. FOREST SCENIC AREA
Mono Lake
Lee Vining
TIOGA PASS ENTRANCE STATION
Tioga Pass
SEE INSET ABOVE
Cherry Lake
Lake Eleanor
Hetch Hetchy Reservoir
YOSEMITE
NATIONAL
PARK
Tuolumne River
Middle Fork
BIG OAK FLAT ENTRANCE STATION
SIERRA
NATIONAL
FOREST
Yosemite Village
El Capitan
Half Dome
Yosemite Valley
Merced River
ANSEL
ADAMS
WILDERNESS
June Lake
to Bridgeport
HOOVER WILDERNESS
Saddlebag Lake
SADDLEBAG LAKE
SADDLEBAG LAKE RD
Tioga Peak 11,526'
INYO
MONO BASIN NATIONAL FOREST SCENIC AREA
POOLE POWER PLANT RD
LOWER LEE VINING
JUNCTION
BIG BEND
ASPEN GROVE
TIOGA LAKE
ELLERY LAKE
MORAINE
BOULDER
CATTLEGUARD
Gaylor Lakes
Dana Plateau
Tioga Pass 9945'
Mt Dana 13,053'
TIOGA RD
YOSEMITE NATIONAL PARK
ANSEL ADAMS WILDERNESS
Mt Gibbs 12,764'
FOREST
28
89
50
395
88
4
108
120
158
167
270

5

Yosemite's Back Door

If you plan to visit both Yosemite and Lake Tahoe in the same trip, the route along the eastern foothills of the Sierra Nevada (Routes 120 East, 395 and 89) can cut your driving distance in half compared to the main highway route west of the mountains (Routes 120 West, 99 and 50). Of course, the driving time may prove to be about the same whichever side of the Sierra you travel, since most of the western route is fast four-lane divided highway, while the eastern route means winding down one mountain road and up another, creeping through small towns and perhaps being lured into side trips to an array of fascinating destinations in one of California's best-hidden regions. Are you ready for a lost-highway adventure? If so, read on.

(The route described in this chapter is inaccessible in winter, when snow closes both Route 120 through Yosemite National Park and Lee Vining Canyon and Route 89 over Monitor Pass.)

sightseeing

The east entrance to Yosemite National Park is located at **Tioga Pass**, about 12 miles from Tuolumne Meadows on Tioga Road (eastbound Route 120). At 9945 feet above sea level, it's the highest automobile pass in California. Upon leaving the park, the road immediately begins a twisting descent, traversing rocky mountain slopes high above the Lee Vining Creek. Streams, lakes and trailheads invite you to pause and savor the wild lands of **Inyo National Forest**. At one scenic overlook you can pull over, pull out your binoculars and see if you can spot some of the bighorn sheep that roam the treacherous slopes on the other side of the canyon. ~ Inyo National Forest, Lee Vining Ranger District, Route 120, Lee Vining; 760-647-3029; e-mail inyovis/r5_inyo@fs.fed.us.

Bodie State Historic Park.

At the mouth of Lee Vining Canyon, Mono Lake comes into view, and soon Route 120 ends at a T-intersection with Route 395. Turn left, and within minutes you'll find yourself in the village of **Lee Vining**, whose 300 residents provide travelers' services or work for the National Forest Service. In the middle of the village, you can get a local's perspective on the battle to save the lake at the **Mono Lake Committee Information Center and Bookstore**, the most complete source for books on the flora, fauna and history of this arid landscape that sits in the rain shadow of the Sierra Nevada. ~ Route 395 at 3rd Street, Lee Vining; 760-647-6595.

No ordinary lake, **Mono Lake** is the saline-alkaline remnant of an ancient inland sea into which seasonal streams have flowed with no outlet; they evaporate and leave alkaline salts

A HIGH-DESERT TIME CAPSULE

The boom town of Bodie thrived for just 11 years, from 1877 to 1888, yet during that time it produced $35 million worth of gold and boasted a population of 10,000—larger than any present-day California town on the east side of the Sierra Nevada. One of the best-preserved ghost towns in the West, **Bodie State Historic Park** is now an open-air museum complete with the homes, shops, churches and saloons of a lost era. Tours are available in summer. Snow often closes the unplowed road to Bodie in winter. Admission. ~ 760-647-6445, fax 760-647-6486; www.seres.ca.gov/sierradsp/bodie, e-mail bodie@qnet.com.

leached from the surrounding desert. The water level has been subsiding, one step forward and two steps back, for countless centuries, causing the excess of minerals in the water to crystallize into spire-shaped calcite "tufa" towers, delicate rock-candy mountains rising from the turquoise water to fringe the shores of the lake with bone-white stalagmites. The process accelerated dramatically throughout the last half of the 20th century as faraway Los Angeles drained water from the streams that fed the lake, lowering its level by 40 feet and doubling its salinity. In 1994, the State Water Board decreed that the water diversion be slowed radically to permanently stabilize the lake level. ~ Route 395; 760-647-3044, fax 760-647-3046; www.monolake.org, e-mail info@monolake.org.

North of the Mono Basin, Route 395 climbs over Conway Summit, a high point in this dry land of creosote, rabbitbrush and sage. Eighteen miles north of Lee Vining, a side road turns off to the east toward **Bodie State Historic Park** (see "A High-desert Time Capsule" on page 103), one of the most interesting historical sights on the east side of the Sierra and well worth the 13-mile, partly paved detour.

Another ten miles on Route 395 bring you to the town of **Bridgeport** near the shore of manmade Bridgeport Reservoir. A cattle-ranching community that began as a supply center for '49 mining camps such as Bodie, Bridgeport has a pretty main street highlighted by the **Mono County Courthouse**, the second-oldest continuously used courthouse in California, dating back to 1880.

Continuing north, Route 395 climbs over 7519-foot Devil's Gate Summit and then descends along the West Walker River, flanked by high white cliffs and strewn

HARLEY HOLIDAY

Bridgeport has a population of about 500—except for one long weekend in late June, when 5000 to 6000 big-bike enthusiasts descend on the town for the **Bridgeport Motorcycle Jamboree**, a raucous celebration featuring concerts and events ranging from street races to a Toys for Tots Parade. No Honda riders, please; the Jamboree is exclusively for Harley-Davidsons. On that weekend, motels are packed to capacity all the way from Lee Vining to Carson City, Nevada.

Opposite: Mono County Courthouse.

with boulders, before entering broad, green Antelope Valley. At the north end of the valley, **Topaz Lake** marks the California–Nevada state line. If you stayed on Route 395, you'd soon find yourself in Carson City, the capitol of Nevada, and just a short distance by fast divided highway from the gambling mecca of Reno. Instead, just past the tiny town of **Topaz** (don't blink or you may miss it), turn left onto Route 89, which climbs steeply into the High Sierra. After 20 miles, the road crests 8314-foot Monitor Pass and emerges into the pine, fir, spruce and aspen stands of **Humboldt-Toiyabe National Forest**. ~ Bridgeport Ranger District, Route 395, Bridgeport; 760-932-7070, fax 775-355-5399; www.fs.fed.us/htnf.

AHHH...

Set against a backdrop of high mountain peaks in a lovely mountain meadow, **Grover Hot Springs State Park** is on an unpaved road that turns off Route 89 to the south at Markleeville. Springs percolate out of the ground at 148 degrees and are cooled to a relaxing 102 to 104 degrees for the park's hot baths and outdoor swimming pool. Take time out to enjoy the springs en route to Lake Tahoe or visit the park as a side trip from South Lake Tahoe, just 25 miles up the road. Closed for two weeks in September. Admission. ~ Off Route 89; 530-694-2248, fax 530-694-2502; www.ceres.ca.gov/sierradsp/grover.html, e-mail grover@gbif.com.

The towns along Route 89 in Alpine County flourished for just two years in the 1860s, when a vein of silver was discovered there and prospectors flooded in to stake their claims. The vein soon played out, and no other silver deposits were ever found in the area. Today the county is almost entirely national forest land and has only 1200 residents, the smallest population of any California county. Almost every road in Alpine County is closed in the winter.

At the crossroads village of Woodfords, Route 89 takes a turn to the left. (If you continued straight, you'd find yourself heading down out of the mountains on Route 88 and soon rejoining Route 395.) Staying on Route 89, you'll soon merge with busy Route 50 for a short, straight descent into the town of **South Lake Tahoe**, the end of this scenic back-door trip from Yosemite to Tahoe.

outdoor adventures

FISHING

Lee Vining Creek, **Tioga Lake** and **Ellery Lake** are stocked with trout weekly during the part of the year that Tioga Pass is open. Some anglers consider these Inyo National Forest options desirable alternatives to streams and lakes inside the Yosemite National Park boundaries, which are not stocked. Much of Ellery Lake's shoreline is too steep and rocky for easy access; Tioga Lake has a trail around it and an easy-to-reach shoreline.

The natural fish population of **Bridgeport Reservoir** was killed off when the lake was drained to keep the water supply flowing for cattle downstream during a drought several years ago, but the lake is well-stocked with rainbow and brown trout and has three boat ramps. For serious anglers, a more intriguing option in the Bridgeport area is **Twin Lakes** in Humboldt-

Bridgeport's main drag.

Toiyabe National Forest (not to be confused with the lakes of the same name south of Lee Vining in Inyo National Forest), world-renowned for its natural population of giant brown trout. These are some savvy fish, though, with years of experience dodging anglers' hooks, so you're more likely to land some of the lakes' planted rainbow trout or kokanee salmon. There are marinas and boat ramps on both lakes and camping nearby. ~ Take Twin Lakes Road south from Bridgeport for about 12 miles.

Topaz Lake offers fishing for rainbow, brown and cutthroat trout from January 1 through September 30. There's a commercial RV park on the California side of the lake and public camping at Douglas County Park on the Nevada side, and if fishing doesn't offer enough opportunity to test your luck, there are two small gaming casinos on the north shore.

Humboldt-Toiyabe National Forest has many fishing lakes accessible from Route 89. Noteworthy among them is **Heenan Lake**, just off the highway halfway between Monitor Pass and Markleeville, offering catch-and-release fishing for rare Lahantan cutthroat trout. Only artificial lures, barbless hooks and electric motors are allowed. Open Friday through Sunday only from Labor Day weekend through the first weekend in October.

Shallow, murky, weedy **Indian Creek Reservoir**, north of Markleeville off Route 89 via Airport Road, used to be a holding pond for South Lake Tahoe sewage effluent. Though no longer used for that purpose, it still gets

HIGH HOPES AND LLAMAS

The Hope Valley along Route 88/89 in Humboldt-Toiyabe National Forest was named by Mormon pioneers, who were searching prayerfully for a passage across the Sierra Nevada. Other valleys nearby are named Faith and Charity. The Mormons never found a route that would let them cross the mountains with covered wagons; today, Route 89 over Monitor Pass is not recommended for travel trailers or large RVs, either. Llamas, however, are a natural option. About once a month during the summer and fall months **Sorensen's Resort** offers llama trips to explore the valley. They last four hours and include a picnic lunch. Sorensen's Resort guests get a discount. Special trips can also be arranged. ~ 14255 Route 88, Hope Valley; 530-694-2203, 800-423-9949; www.sorensensresort.com.

Tufa formations at Mono Lake.

smelly in summer due to algae blooms. So, with all the pristine alpine lakes in the vicinity, why would anyone choose to fish here? The rich food chain makes for an abundance of trophy-size rainbow trout. White pelicans also flock here—a good indication of good fishing.

HIKING

Visitors can walk the quarter-mile paved trail to some of Mono Lake's most bizarre tufa formations at **Mono Lake South Tufa Reserve**. ~ Five miles southeast of Lee Vining off Route 120; 760-647-3046; www.monolake.org, e-mail info@monolake.org.

Of the many possibilities for hiking in Humboldt-Toiyabe National Forest, the most accessible trails start at **Grover Hot Springs State Park** and head into the surrounding forested hills. One of the prettiest goes for about a mile up **Hot Springs Creek** to a waterfall that spills out of the pines into rivulets down a near-vertical granite face.

CAMPING

Outside Yosemite National Park, several small Inyo National Forest campgrounds are found along Route 120 as it makes the long, steep 4000-foot descent from the High Sierra to the sagebrush desert around Mono Lake. These camps offer a reasonable alternative when the high-country campgrounds of Yosemite's Tuolumne Meadows area are packed to overflowing— which, in camping season, is most of the time. Although these campgrounds are more than two hours' drive from Yosemite Valley, any of them can make a convenient base for exploring the park's northern high country as well as the strange shoreline of Mono Lake.

Tioga Lake Campground, the closest national forest campground to Yosemite's east entrance, just a mile outside the park, is situated well below highway level and a short distance from pretty Tioga Lake, whose shoreline trail makes for a good sunset walk. It's small—just 13 tent/RV sites—and fills up quickly with weekend anglers and overflow campers from the national park. At 9700 feet elevation, it can be cold and windy. Drinking water and vault toilets are available, but no hookups. Sites cost $15 per night, first-come, first-served. Open June to mid-October. ~ Route 120; 760-647-3044.

Junction Campground, four miles outside the park, has 13 tent/RV sites in an open area at the junction of Route 120 and Saddlebag Road. There are vault toilets but no drinking water or hookups. Sites cost $9 per night, first-come, first-served. Open June to mid-October. ~ Route 120; 760-647-3044.

Saddlebag Lake Campground is set at just over 10,000 feet, near the shore of the highest-altitude lake in California that can be reached by road. The surrounding area is mostly slanted slabs of bare granite with a few pines struggling for survival at timberline. There are 20 tent/RV sites as well as a group site; RVers soon discover that few of these sites are level. Besides drinking water and vault toilets, facilities include a boat launch ramp and a store that sells groceries and rents boats; no hookups. Sites cost $15 per night, first-come, first-served. Open June to mid-October. ~ From Route 120, turn north at Junction Campground and drive north for two miles on the mostly unpaved road; 760-647-3044, group reservations 877-444-6777.

WINTER WORKOUT

If you enjoy working up a sweat in the snow, or better yet, prefer the isolation of backcountry wilderness in the winter, **The Hope Valley Outdoor Center** offers 60 kilometers of backcountry trails during the winter months. Some are groomed, others aren't. Those who prefer not going it alone can join others in a guided tour. Other winter activities include snowmobiling and telemarking as well as dog sled tours and sleigh rides. There's a wood-fired sauna on the premises and the folks are as friendly as can be. Besides, the center is close to Grover Hot Springs, where you can soak away all those muscles sore from skiing. ~ 14255 Route 88/89, Hope Valley; 530-694-2203.

Ellery Lake Campground is at an elevation of 9500 feet, three miles down Route 120 from Tioga Lake. It has just 12 tent/RV sites, with drinking water and flush toilets but no hookups. Sites cost $15 per night, first-come, first-served. Open June to mid-October. ~ Route 120; 760-647-3044.

Big Bend Campground, at 7800 feet the lowest in elevation of the Inyo National Forest campgrounds along Lee Vining Creek, offers 17 tent/RV sites with dramatic views of the Sierra Nevada's steep eastern slope towering overhead. It has drinking water and vault toilets, but no hookups. Sites cost $15 per night, first-come, first-served. Open late April to mid-October. ~ From Route 120, turn north at the marked road 8.5 miles down the canyon from the national park entrance or 3.5 miles upcanyon from the Route 395 highway junction; drive three miles to the campground; 760-647-3044.

The Mono County Building and Parks Department also maintains several campgrounds along Poole Power Plant Road, at the lower end of Lee Vining Canyon off Route 120, nine miles east of the national park entrance and three miles from

Hope Valley.

the highway junction with Route 395. Facilities are minimal, with outhouses but no hookups. **Aspen Grove Campground** is the largest of the county campgrounds, with 58 tent/RV sites along Lee Vining Creek at an elevation of 7500 feet. Well water is available at Aspen Grove. The entrance to **Moraine Campground**, with 30 tent/RV sites but no water, is about five miles up the same road. **Boulder Campground**, half a mile farther up Poole Power Plant Road, has 22 tent/RV sites but no water. **Cattleguard Campground**, located close to where Poole Power Plant Road turns off Route 120, has 16 tent/RV sites. There's no water, but the view makes up for it. Sites at all four campgrounds cost $8 per night, first-come, first-served. Open May through October. ~ Poole Power Plant Road; 760-932-5451.

Half a mile down Route 120 from the Poole Power Plant Road turnoff, the creekside **Lower Lee Vining Campground** is also operated by Mono County. It has 59 tent/RV sites with outhouses but no drinking water. Sites cost $8 per night, first-come, first-served. Open May through October. ~ Route 120; 760-932-5451.

Grover Hot Springs State Park has 76 tent/RV sites in two campgrounds within walking distance of the pools. The shady setting, surrounded on three sides by mountain slopes robed with evergreens, couldn't be more idyllic. Sites cost $12 per night. Reservations (800-444-7275) are essential from about May 15 to Labor Day; during the rest of the year sites are first-come, first-served. ~ Off Route 89; 530-694-2248, fax 530-694-2502; www.ceres.ca.gov/sierradsp/grover.html, e-mail grover@gbif.com.

lodging

Just outside the east entrance of Yosemite National Park, **Tioga Pass Resort** has ten rustic log cabins and four motel-style rooms in the main lodge. The cabins have kitchens and rent by the week. Though simple, these accommodations are almost luxurious compared to any place you can stay inside the national park in the Tioga Road/Tuolumne Meadows area, and the setting, with its views of high mountains and the vertical walls of Lee Vining Canyon, couldn't be more magnificent. Summer season runs from mid-May to mid-October; winter season runs from the week before Christmas to May. ~ Route 120, Lee Vining; 209-372-4471; www.tiogapassresort.com. BUDGET TO MODERATE.

Lee Vining has quite a few motels for a town of only 300 people. One good bet is **Murphey's Lodging**, with 43 spacious, modern rooms, some with kitchenettes. Most rooms are qui-

Wetting Your Whistle

Frankly, there's not much going on in this neck of the woods once the sun sets, but the Irish-style pub in the **Bridgeport Inn** is the liveliest spot in the valley after dark. Its long, polished wood bar was originally the clerk's counter in the county courthouse down the street. Entertainment consists of a jukebox stocked with '50s and '60s rock. ~ 205 Main Street, Bridgeport; 760-932-7380, fax 760-932-1160; www.thebridgeportinn.com. The **Cutthroat Saloon** in Markleeville was presumably named after the trout, but then again, you can never be quite sure. Occupying the former Alpine Hotel from the town's short-lived mining boom days, it's a legendary biker-friendly saloon where curious travelers can order a beer or a shot of tequila and bend an elbow in the company of desperados, rebels and weekend road warriors. ~ Route 89 at Montgomery Street, Markleeville; 530-694-2150.

Cabin at Sorensen's Resort.

etly located well back from the highway. Guests enjoy the use of a sauna and jacuzzi, and for anglers there are fish cleaning and freezing facilities. ~ Route 395, Lee Vining; 760-647-6316; www.murpheysyosemite.com, e-mail info@yosemitemur pheys.com. MODERATE.

Upon arriving at the historic **Bridgeport Inn**, a white-shingle building dating back to 1877, you enter a parlor with a gleaming chandelier and a big wood stove. Most of the simply decorated rooms feature Monterey furniture, a collectible style handcrafted from the 1920s to the 1940s. An upstairs suite once occupied by Mark Twain is restored with authentic Victorian-era antiques. Closed mid-December through February. ~ 205 Main Street, Bridgeport; 760-932-7380, fax 760-932-1160; www.thebridgeportinn.com, e-mail reservations@thebridge portinn.com. MODERATE.

In the high country of Alpine County, **Sorensen's Resort** offers accommodations in 30 rustic cabins scattered amid stands of quaking aspen. Most have kitchen facilities, eight have fireplaces and private decks, and one has a hot tub. ~ 14255 Route 88/89, Hope Valley; 530-694-2203, 800-423-9949; www. sorensensresort.com. MODERATE TO ULTRA-DELUXE.

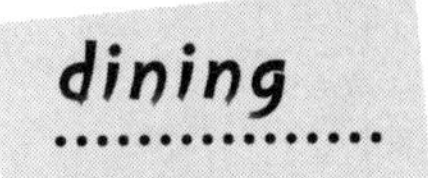

The unpretentious little restaurant at **Tioga Pass Resort** serves three meals daily, with a menu that ranges from soup and sandwiches to full dinners and homemade pies. Closed mid-October to Memorial Day. ~ Route 120, Lee Vining; 209-372-4471; www.tiogapassresort.com. BUDGET TO MODERATE.

You won't encounter many restaurants along the route described in this chapter. Perhaps the most interesting possibility is the **Bridgeport Inn** with its white linen tablecloths and Main Street view. The menu features steaks, rack of lamb, salmon and Alaskan king crab legs, as well as California and imported wines. Closed mid-December through February. ~ 205 Main Street, Bridgeport; 760-932-7380; www.thebridgeportinn.com. MODERATE.

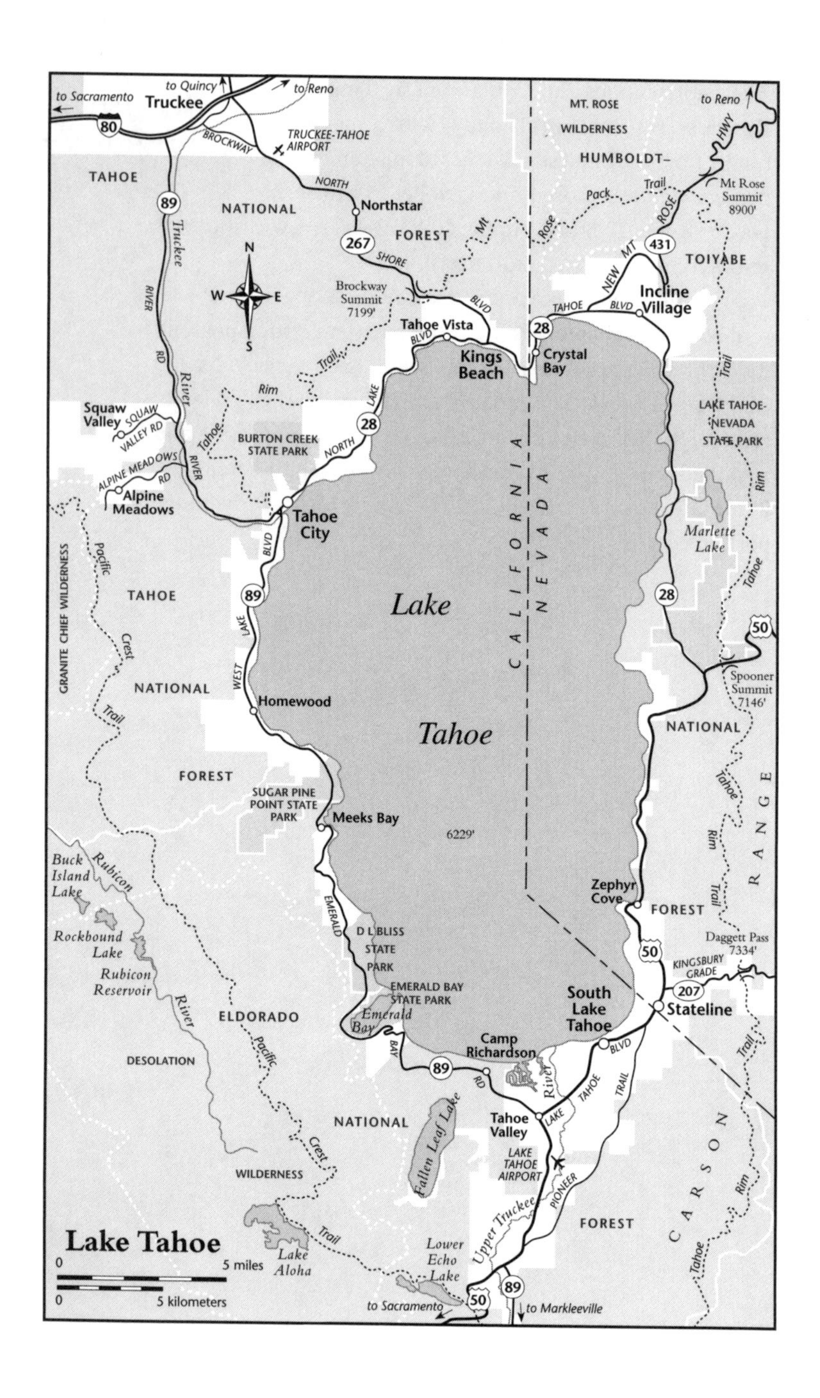

Lake Tahoe
to Quincy
to Sacramento
Truckee
to Reno
80
BROCKWAY
TRUCKEE-TAHOE AIRPORT
MT. ROSE
WILDERNESS
HUMBOLDT–
TOIYABE
to Reno
HWY
Mt Rose Summit 8900'
TAHOE
NATIONAL
FOREST
89
Truckee
RIVER
RD
River
NORTH
Northstar
267
SHORE
Brockway Summit 7199'
BLVD
Tahoe Vista
Kings Beach
28
Crystal Bay
TAHOE
BLVD
NEW MT ROSE
431
Incline Village
Pack Trail
Mt Rose
Tahoe Rim Trail
Squaw Valley
SQUAW VALLEY RD
ALPINE MEADOWS RD
Alpine Meadows
BURTON CREEK STATE PARK
NORTH LAKE
Tahoe City
LAKE TAHOE-NEVADA STATE PARK
Marlette Lake
CALIFORNIA
NEVADA
Lake
Tahoe
6229'
GRANITE CHIEF WILDERNESS
Pacific Crest Trail
WEST LAKE BLVD
Homewood
50
Spooner Summit 7146'
NATIONAL
FOREST
RANGE
SUGAR PINE POINT STATE PARK
Meeks Bay
Buck Island Lake
Rubicon
Rockbound Lake
Rubicon Reservoir
River
EMERALD
D L BLISS STATE PARK
EMERALD BAY STATE PARK
Emerald Bay
BAY
Zephyr Cove
Daggett Pass 7334'
KINGSBURY GRADE
207
Stateline
South Lake Tahoe
Camp Richardson
BLVD
ELDORADO
DESOLATION
WILDERNESS
NATIONAL
Fallen Leaf Lake
Tahoe Valley
LAKE TAHOE
TRAIL
LAKE TAHOE AIRPORT
PIONEER
Upper Truckee
CARSON
FOREST
Lake Aloha
Lower Echo Lake
to Sacramento
to Markleeville
0
5 miles
5 kilometers

PART 2

California's Mountain Playground: Lake Tahoe

Lake Tahoe is North America's largest alpine lake, 22 miles long and 12 miles wide, and the third-deepest lake in North America—1557 feet. Only Crater Lake in Oregon and Lake Atitlán in Guatemala are deeper. The water in the lake's depths remains a constant 39 degrees year-round and prevents the surface from freezing in winter. Lake Tahoe contains approximately 40,000,000,000,000 gallons of water—enough to cover the entire land area of California in water 14 inches deep. The amount of water that evaporates off the lake's surface could supply the entire water usage of a city the size of Los Angeles if it could somehow be recaptured. Like Yosemite Valley, Old Faithful or the Grand Canyon, Lake Tahoe stands high on the list of western America's natural wonders.

But there's something different about Lake Tahoe from these other attractions. Thanks to private entrepreneurs, three national forests and two state park systems, Lake Tahoe offers a wider array of outdoor recreation options year-round than almost any other travel destination in the West. On the water, you can kayak, scoot along on a Waverunner, waterski or parasail, fish for the lake's legendary giant Mackinaw trout or take a sunset dinner cruise on a glass-bottomed sailboat. Along the shore, you can play one of over a dozen golf courses, ride horseback or rollerblade along paved trails that follow the water's edge for miles. You can trek deep into the High Sierra's most remote wilderness. And in winter, the Tahoe Basin boasts the biggest and best alpine ski slopes in California, as well as the longest total mileage of cross-country ski trails.

Visitors to Lake Tahoe have the widest possible range of restaurant and lodging choices available. In general, the biggest hotels are found at Stateline casino resorts and at Squaw Valley's ski village. The majority of small, luxurious

OPPOSITE: Fanette Island in Emerald Bay.

bed-and-breakfast accommodations are also found near ski areas, especially Heavenly Lake Tahoe on the South Shore. More rustic lodging is found along the North Shore. And if you prefer historic hotels, try Camp Richardson, Truckee or Crystal Bay. There are public campgrounds on all four sides of the lake and restaurants for every taste and pocketbook. Nightlife is mainly centered in the casino districts of Crystal Bay and Stateline.

One of the most remarkable Lake Tahoe phenomena is that each of the four sides of the lake is different. The South Shore has the largest population, the most marinas, the biggest gaming casinos and one of the biggest ski areas, as well as the most hotel beds. The West Shore offers natural beauty, historic sites and wilderness access. On the North Shore you'll find small towns with small lodgings and restaurants—just down the road from one of America's biggest and most famous ski resorts, Squaw Valley. And on the East Side, you'll find a shoreline that was once clearcut by pioneers and now offers golf courses and a Western theme park side-by-side with the largest and least developed state park on the lake. With so many possibilities open to visitors, the biggest challenge involved in a Lake Tahoe vacation may be deciding what to do first.

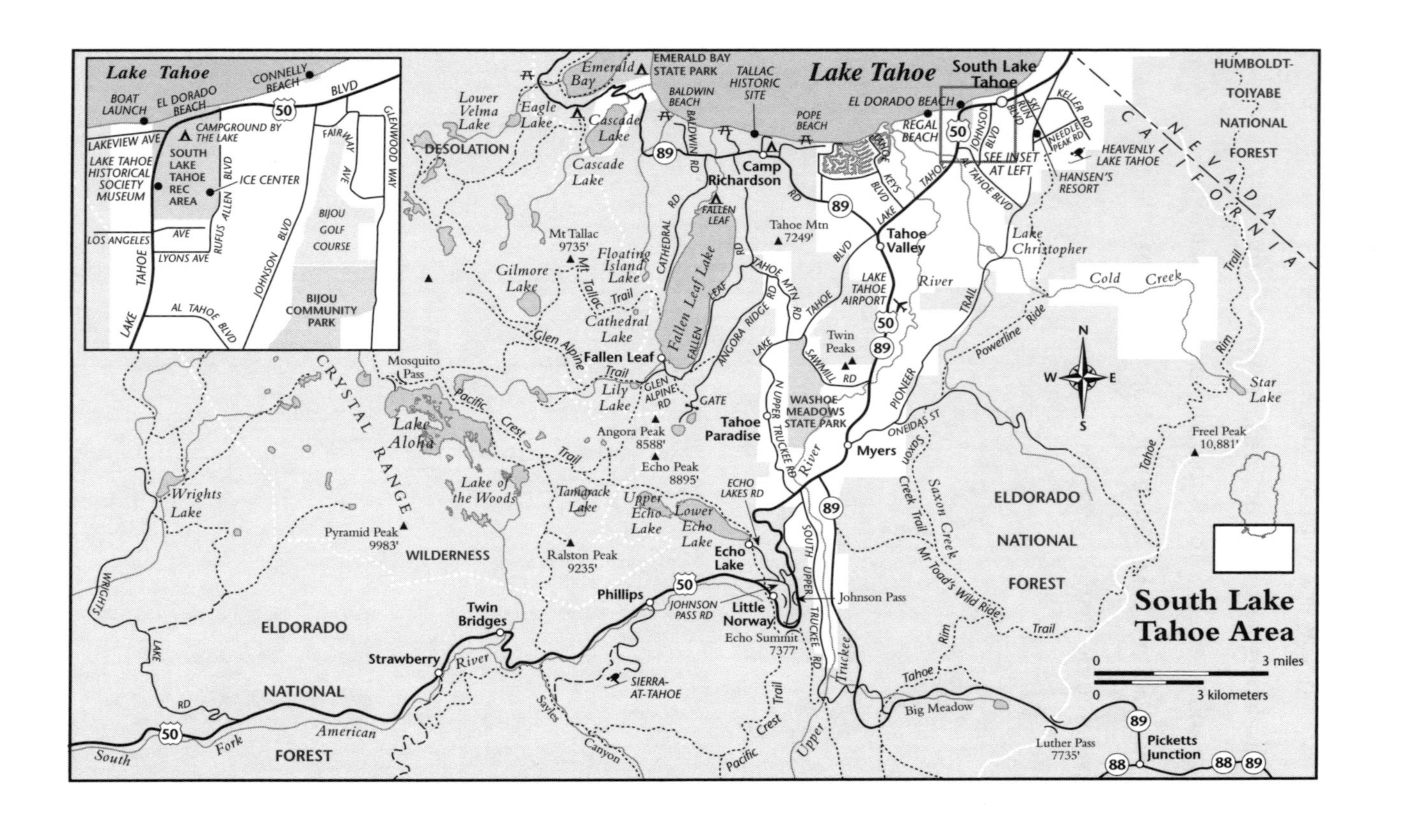

South Lake Tahoe Area
Lake Tahoe
South Lake Tahoe
EMERALD BAY STATE PARK
TALLAC HISTORIC SITE
BALDWIN BEACH
POPE BEACH
EL DORADO BEACH
REGAL BEACH
SEE INSET AT LEFT
HEAVENLY LAKE TAHOE
HANSEN'S RESORT
KELLER RD
SKI RUN BLVD
NEEDLE PEAK RD
JOHNSON BLVD
AL TAHOE BLVD
TAHOE KEYS BLVD
LAKE TAHOE BLVD
HUMBOLDT-TOIYABE NATIONAL FOREST
NEVADA
CALIFORNIA
Emerald Bay
Lower Velma Lake
Eagle Lake
Cascade Lake
DESOLATION
WILDERNESS
Camp Richardson
BALDWIN RD
FALLEN LEAF
Tahoe Mtn 7249'
Tahoe Valley
Lake Christopher
Mt Tallac 9735'
Mt Tallac Trail
Floating Island Lake
Gilmore Lake
Cathedral Lake
CATHEDRAL RD
Fallen Leaf Lake
FALLEN LEAF RD
TAHOE MTN RD
ANGORA RIDGE RD
LAKE TAHOE AIRPORT
River
TRAIL
Cold Creek
Glen Alpine Trail
Fallen Leaf
Mosquito Pass
CRYSTAL RANGE
Lily Lake
GLEN ALPINE RD
GATE
Twin Peaks
SAWMILL RD
WASHOE MEADOWS STATE PARK
N UPPER TRUCKEE RD
Tahoe Paradise
Powerline Ride
PIONEER
Rim Trail
Star Lake
Lake Aloha
Pacific Crest Trail
Angora Peak 8588'
Echo Peak 8895'
Myers
ONEIDAS ST
Freel Peak 10,881'
Tahoe
Wrights Lake
Lake of the Woods
Tamarack Lake
Upper Echo Lake
Lower Echo Lake
ECHO LAKES RD
Saxon Creek Trail
Saxon Creek
Mr Toad's Wild Ride
ELDORADO NATIONAL FOREST
Pyramid Peak 9983'
Ralston Peak 9235'
Echo Lake
SOUTH UPPER TRUCKEE RD
Johnson Pass
Phillips
JOHNSON PASS RD
Little Norway
Echo Summit 7377'
WRIGHTS LAKE RD
Twin Bridges
Strawberry
River
SIERRA-AT-TAHOE
Sayles Canyon
Tahoe Rim Trail
Upper Truckee
Big Meadow
South Fork American River
Luther Pass 7735'
Picketts Junction
0
3 miles
0
3 kilometers
N
S
E
W
50
89
88
Lake Tahoe
BOAT LAUNCH
EL DORADO BEACH
CONNELLY BEACH
BLVD
CAMPGROUND BY THE LAKE
LAKEVIEW AVE
LAKE TAHOE HISTORICAL SOCIETY MUSEUM
SOUTH LAKE TAHOE REC AREA
ICE CENTER
RUFUS ALLEN BLVD
FAIRWAY AVE
GLENWOOD WAY
BIJOU GOLF COURSE
JOHNSON BLVD
LOS ANGELES AVE
LYONS AVE
LAKE TAHOE
AL TAHOE BLVD
BIJOU COMMUNITY PARK

6

South Lake Tahoe

With a population of 21,000, South Lake Tahoe is the largest town on Lake Tahoe—bigger, in fact, than all the other communities on the lake combined. It has, however, had its share of economic ups and downs in the century or so since it sprung up as a supply station for long-vanished resorts along the lakeshore. After Lake Tahoe's glamour shifted to the North Shore, seduced by the fame that the 1960 Olympics brought to Squaw Valley, the South Shore found itself sliding into genteel decrepitude, its main street lined with seedy motels whose worn carpeting spoke of bygone glory days. Today, though, all that has changed so much that if you haven't visited South Lake Tahoe for a few years, you may hardly recognize it.

South Lake Tahoe is now swept up in a billion-dollar redevelopment project, designed by a coalition of businesspeople, environmentalists, politicians, land developers, scientists, futurists and ordinary citizens. Half of this sum is going into accommodations and improvements for Heavenly Lake Tahoe, a big-time ski resort rivaling Squaw Valley. There are improved parks and beaches, new shopping centers, a 91,000-square-foot convention center and a planned environmental learning and outdoor recreation complex centered around a two-acre replica of Lake Tahoe. True, there are still a few threadbare little mom-and-pop motels along the main drag, but the municipality is doing its best to make sure you're too dazzled to notice them.

South Lake Tahoe is bounded on the west and east by two key landmarks that locals often mention when giving directions. At the west end of town, the intersection where Emerald Bay Drive turns north off Route 50 for the scenic drive up the lake's west shore (see Chapter 7) is known as "the Y." At the east end, the Nevada state line marks the city limit of South Lake Tahoe; the town keeps on going—all night, actually—with the big Stateline casinos just over the imaginary border. By far the tallest buildings around, they're visible from anywhere on the south part of the lake.

sightseeing

The natural place to begin your South Lake Tahoe experience is the **Scenic Gondola at Heavenly**, an 11.5- to 18-minute ride that carries you 3000 feet up the mountainside for an astonishing 360-degree view of the lake and the Sierra Nevada that lays the town out before you like a map. The 138 gondola cabins on the five-mile steel cable are capable of carrying more than 5700 passengers an hour, so you'll rarely have to wait long. Take your time at the top, where you'll find an observation deck, picnic areas and hiking trailheads. The lower gondola station is located on Lake Tahoe Boulevard (Route 50) just a block west of the Nevada state line. The Nifty Fifty Trolley can pick you up anywhere in South Lake Tahoe and take you to the gondola. All-day gondola tickets cost only a few dollars more than single rides. ~ Heavenly Ski Area; 775-586-7000; www.skiheavenly.com.

Scenic Gondola at Heavenly.

The **Lake Tahoe Historical Society Museum**, next door to the South Lake Tahoe Chamber of Commerce information center, offers a peek at the area's early days. There are baskets, dolls and many arrowheads made by the Washoe Indians, who used to make the Tahoe Basin their home during the summer months and migrate down to the Carson Valley in winter. Also on display are a collection of vintage ski equipment, exhibits about the Pony Express and the logging operations during Nevada's Comstock Lode silver boom, and photographs of old-time South Shore resort hotels and the steamships that brought guests there from Tahoe City. A video shows clips from early movies shot at Lake Tahoe. Behind the museum are the oldest cabin in the region and an 1859 tollhouse. Open mid-June through Labor Day weekend. Admission. ~ 3058 Lake Tahoe Boulevard, South Lake Tahoe; 530-541-5458.

A large municipal park in the center of town, **Bijou Community Park** has group picnic shelters, restrooms and a gazebo bandstand, as well as a full array of recreational facilities including a children's playground, sand volleyball courts, basketball courts, horseshoe pits, a skateboard park and an archery range. ~ Tahoe Boulevard at Johnson Boulevard; 530-542-6056.

South Lake Tahoe's shoreline has several marinas and three public beaches. **El Dorado Beach** is a sandy pocket beach with a sweeping view of the lake. It's located in the center of town, with no dunes to provide privacy from the busy highway a few yards away, so you'll only want to consider sunbathing there if the stares of passing motorists don't make you feel self-conscious. ~ Route 50 at Lakeview Avenue.

Half a mile west of El Dorado Beach, **Regan Beach** is broad and family-oriented, with volleyball courts, playground equipment, picnic tables, barbecue grills and food concessions, though not much sand. Most of the waterfront "beach" is landscaped with lawns and shade trees. ~ On Lakeview Avenue at Sacramento Street.

Connelly Beach, tucked away just off Route 50 behind Timber Cove Lodge is a small, sandy beach with picnic tables and restrooms. It fronts a shallow swimming area where the water is relatively warm in summer. ~ 3411 Lake Tahoe Boulevard; 530-542-6056.

outdoor adventures

HIKING

Most of the great hiking trails near South Lake Tahoe are past the west edge of town off Emerald Bay Road (see Chapter 7). In town, most old South Shore trails have been widened, paved and given street names. Distances for all trails are one way unless otherwise noted. For a short hike with an unforgettable view, ride the Heavenly Gondola (fee) to the start of the **Tahoe Vista Trail**, a 1.1-mile walk along a 9000-foot ridgeline. The first part of the trail goes through evergreen forest; then it breaks out onto a more open expanse, where switch-

View from Tahoe Rim Trail.

Tahoe Trekking

The ultimate hike, on the South Shore as everywhere else around the lake, is the magnificent **Tahoe Rim Trail**. Completed in 2001 after a 20-year, all-volunteer effort, the 165-mile trek has now joined the John Muir and Pacific Crest trails in making California a world-class destination for long-distance trekkers. Passing through three national forests and merging with the Pacific Crest Trail to cross the rugged Desolation Wilderness, the trail can be reached from nine major trailheads with road access and parking areas, ranging from 12 to 32 miles apart. It is open to hikers and horseback riders. Most parts of the trail can also be used with mountain bikes; all wheeled vehicles are prohibited in wilderness areas and on the Pacific Crest Trail, however, as well as on two segments of the trail on the northeast side of the lake (one of which can be bypassed by biking the legendary Flume Trail—see Chapter 9). Just to confuse matters further, one segment of the trail south of Mount Rose is open to bikes only on even-numbered dates.

The main drawback for casual day-hikers on the Tahoe Rim Trail is that most of the roads where the trailheads are located cross over the lowest points on the rim, so the first several miles of a hike from any access point typically involve an ambitious climb to the higher ridges. You can make private arrangements for a dropoff at one trailhead and a pickup at the next. One of the two main trailheads near South Lake Tahoe is **Big Meadow**, on Route 89 about five miles south of the edge of town. You can hike in either direction, but the better bet is to head south from the parking area. The first part of the trail, the 2.5-mile hike to **Round Lake**, is steep and strenuous. The pretty alpine lake beneath the crags of the Carson Range makes a great day-hike destination by itself, or you can continue south for another mile to **Meiss Lake**, set in a forest glen at 8400 feet. ~ Tahoe Rim Trail Association, 297 Kingsbury Grade, Stateline; 775-588-0686; www.tahoerimtrail.org, e-mail info@tahoerimtrail.org.

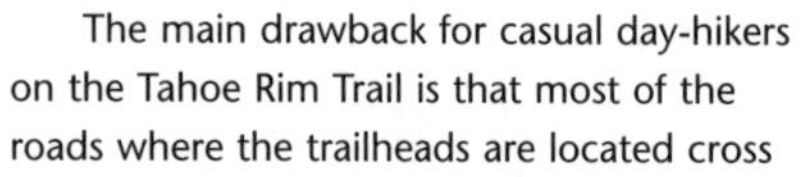

backs take you up through a boulder field for the ultimate overview. ~ Heavenly Ski Area; 775-586-7000; www.skiheavenly.com.

Hiking the entire 165-mile **Tahoe Rim Trail** around the lake would take well over a week, but segments from all trailheads make for good out-and-back hikes. See "Tahoe Trekking" sidebar for more information.

The Tahoe Rim Trail merges with the **Pacific Crest Trail** south of Meiss Lake and then doubles back northward, but if you plan to go farther west, the better plan is to join the Pacific Crest/Tahoe Rim trail at the **Echo Lakes Trailhead**, located off Route 50 southwest of South Lake Tahoe. Drive to the Johnson Pass summit, turn off to the right at Johnson Pass Sno-Park, and make another right turn on Echo Lakes Road, which brings you to two parking areas near the Echo Chalet and marina. The Pacific Crest/Tahoe Rim Trail follows the north shoreline of Lower and Upper Echo Lakes for about two miles (you can bypass this leg of the hike by taking a water taxi from the marina to the dock on the upper lake). Shortly after, the trail crosses into the **Desolation Wilderness** of Eldorado National Forest. Two miles from Upper Echo Lake (four miles from the trailhead) will bring you to **Tamarack Lake**, a classic mountain lake encircled by dense forest at the base of 9235-foot Ralston Peak. Beyond this point, the trail enters a broad basin flanked on all sides by the granite peaks of the Crystal Range and filled with dozens of large and small lakes. A labyrinth of side trails head off toward **Lake of the Woods** (.5 mile from the main trail), **Lake Margery** and **Lake Lucille** (1 mile from the main trail) and other sparkling little alpine lakes. But the real showpiece of the basin is **Lake Aloha**, six miles from the Echo Lakes Trailhead. It's right on the main trail, which follows the north shore of the lake before heading off over switch-back-steep Mosquito Pass and down

INDOOR SPORTS

Okay, let's face it—Lake Tahoe weather isn't *always* perfect. If you find yourself in South Lake Tahoe on a cold, blustery day when you don't feel like hiking or kayaking for fear the wind will carry your hat away, and you don't feel like taking the kids on a tour of local art galleries and casinos, why not try the **South Lake Tahoe Recreation & Swim Pool Complex**? There you'll find a year-round swimming pool, a complete weight room and gymnasium, and an assortment of programs including aerobics classes and daily supervised activities for children and teens. It's also a great place to meet some genuine Lake Tahoe locals. Admission. ~ 1180 Rufus Allen Boulevard; 530-542-6056; www.ci.south-lake-tahoe.ca.us, e-mail recreation@ci.south-lake-tahoe.ca.us.

into the forbidding reaches of Rockbound Valley. Lake Aloha is a manmade reservoir that provides drinking water for the city of Sacramento, but despite its unnatural origin, it's a breathtaking sight, two miles long and a mile wide, polka-dotted with literally hundreds of tiny, bare rock islands. ~ Eldorado National Forest, Lake Tahoe Basin Management Unit; 530-573-2600; www.r5.fs.fed.us/ltbmu.

BIKING

One of the most famous mountain bike trails in the Lake Tahoe region, **Mr. Toad's Wild Ride** is a thrill-a-minute downhill ride for skilled mountain bikers only. Following Saxon Creek down a deep, steep valley, it plunges 2200 feet in just three miles. Wear a helmet and protective gear! Start by taking Route 89 south of town for about five miles to the Big Meadow parking area, a trailhead for the Tahoe Rim

Trail. Ride two and a half miles northeast along the rim trail, a strenuous uphill climb that leaves you poised at the start of Mr. Toad's ride. Take a left and hang on. The ride ends at Oneidas Street near the Lake Tahoe Airport. Turn left to return to Route 89 or right to continue into town on the much easier three-mile **Powerline Ride**.

If Mr. Toad's ride sounds a little too wild, another short, challenging up-and-down route close to town is the **Twin Peaks Off-Road Trail**. It climbs 600 feet to a vantage point near the east summit of the 7100-foot peaks for a great lake view. *Caution*: The first part of the trail is a favorite haunt of motorized all-terrain vehicle riders.

For a longer ride, you can take the **Tahoe Rim Trail** east as far as you wish from the Big Meadow parking area on southbound Route 89. (You can't ride far west from Big Meadow because the rim trail merges with the Pacific Crest Trail, on which bicycles are prohibited.) It's 22.5 miles, all spectacular, from Big Meadow to the next trailhead at Kingsbury Grade on the Nevada side of the lake. You'll quickly discover that the Big Meadow trailhead, like all access points along the 165-mile trail, is a low spot on the rim, so the first few miles of the trip involve a strenuous climb with an elevation gain of more than 2300 feet. Beyond that, it's a mellower ride along the slope of 10,881-foot Freel Peak, the highest mountain on the Lake Tahoe rim, to Star Lake, about 14 miles from the Big Meadows trailhead.

Mountain bikes are for rent at **Lakeview Sports** (3131 Lake Tahoe Boulevard; 530-544-0183), **Tahoe Bike Shop** (2277 Lake Tahoe Boulevard; 530-544-8060), **CyclePaths** (11785

MAKING A SPLASH

Can't resist the call of the water? All South Lake Tahoe marinas rent water skis, and most also rent wetsuits, wakeboards and kneeboards. If you don't know how to do it, you can arrange for water-skiing instruction at **Werley's Water Ski School**, located at the Tahoe Keys Marina. ~ 2345 Venice Drive East, South Lake Tahoe; 530-544-5099. To combine your water skiing or boating adventure with high-flying thrills, arrange a parasailing ride at **Ski Run Boat Company**. ~ 900 Ski Run Boulevard; 530-544-0200. At **Action Watersports of Tahoe**, you can parasail without getting wet, lifting off from shore or from the deck of the tow boat. After flying you like a kite, the boat reels you in to land on deck. ~ Timber Cove Marina; 530-541-7245.

West Lake Boulevard; 530-581-1171) and **Anderson's Bicycle Rental** (645 Emerald Bay Road; 530-541-0500).

BOATING

Boating of all types is, naturally enough, the most popular summer activity on Lake Tahoe. In 2001, the Tahoe Regional Planning Agency banned certain types of gasoline-powered boat from the lake to reduce air pollution, so owners of older boats and personal watercraft should check with the TRPA (775-558-4547; ceres.ca.gov/trpa) before hauling them up to the lake. The new restrictions also provide for no-wake zones (5 mph speed limit) within 600 feet of the shoreline, making kayaking a more enjoyable experience than it used to be. Although opponents of the new restrictions voiced concerns that they would discourage boaters and hurt the area's hospitality industry, you'll see that their worries were unfounded if you visit the lake on a summer weekend, when boat traffic seems almost bumper-to-bumper. Boating is a whole different experience during the week, when most craft remain moored at the docks.

You'll find a wide range of watercraft for rent, from paddleboats, canoes and kayaks to Sea Doos and Wave Runners, pontoon boats, sailboats and powerboats suitable for water skiing, and even 50-foot yachts, at South Lake Tahoe's public marinas—from west to east along the lakefront: **Lakeside Marina** (4041 Lakeshore Boulevard; 530-541-6626), **Ski Run Marina Village** (900 Ski Run Boulevard; 530-544-0200), **Timber Cove Marina** (3411 Lake Tahoe Boulevard; 530-544-2942)

ADDICTED TO FUN

Offering a different approach to Lake Tahoe adventuring, **The Funaddicts** are a somewhat fluid company of local folks who can share a full range of experiences with you for a fee. The group is organized around a long-time sailing captain who offers day charters on his sailboat, and members present an array of other activities including kayaking, wildlife viewing, wakeboarding and waterskiing, tubing, boat camping and hiking. They will arrange to pick you up at any spot on the Lake Tahoe waterfront. ~ 530-544-6947, or call the boat at 530-308-5125; www.funaddictsonline.com, e-mail kimo@tahoe.com.

115

Cruising the Lake

No survey of outdoor fun on Lake Tahoe would be complete without considering the cruise boats that have been an institution on Lake Tahoe since the days before the lake could be reached by road. **Hornblower Cruises** runs the *Tahoe Queen,* the only authentic paddlewheeler now operating on the lake. Options include family dinner cruises or three-hour dinner/dance cruises on Saturdays year-round, Fridays through Mondays from early April to mid-October, as well as daily scenic cruises along the shoreline to Emerald Bay on the West Shore year-round. Reservations are required. ~ 900 Ski Run Boulevard; 530-541-3364, 800-238-2463; www.hornblower.com.

Tahoe ParaDice Charters runs sightseeing trips to Vikingsholm from Camp Richardson in the summer and Tahoe Keys Marina in winter. They also offer party cruises and can arrange for live entertainment or an onboard hot tub. ~ 530-541-7499.

For a smaller-scale cruise experience, step aboard the ***Balderdash***, a replica of a 1940s tugboat. This tour company offers private breakfast or dinner cruises to Emerald Bay for small groups. ~ 530-542-8713. The **Tahoe Schooner Company** takes groups to Emerald Bay on a 1931 sailing schooner. ~ Tahoe Keys Marina; 530-542-2217, 888-550-4575; e-mail tahoeschooner@webtv.net. **My Friend with a Boat** offers half-day, full-day, sunset and overnight custom cruises for private parties of up to six people. Private clothing-optional sunbathing is okay. ~ 775-588-6716; www.myfriendwithaboat.com.

and **Tahoe Keys Marina** (Tahoe Keys Boulevard at Venice Drive; 530-544-8888). All four marinas have launch ramps for private boats.

There is also a municipal boat launch ramp at **El Dorado Beach**. ~ Route 50 at Lakeview Avenue; 530-542-6056.

Tahoe is not the only lake in the vicinity where you can enjoy boating. Rentals are available on Fallen Leaf Lake at **Fallen Leaf Marina**. ~ 400 Fallen Leaf Road; 530-544-0787.

GOLF

Of the two dozen Lake Tahoe area golf courses that are open to the public, only five are on the South Shore—three in South Lake Tahoe and two in Stateline (see Chapter 9). Competition for tee times can be stiff.

The oldest golf course at Lake Tahoe, the nine-hole **Bijou Golf Course** dates back to 1920, when it served luxury resorts in the area. Short (2031 yards) but challenging (32 par), this inexpensive municipal course in the center of town is known for its water hazards, fed by a natural creek that meanders among the fairways. Cart and club rentals are available. Tee times are first-come, first-served. Open May through October. ~ 3464 Fairway at Johnson Boulevard; 530-542-6097.

Tahoe Paradise Golf Course, the first 18-hole golf course at Lake Tahoe, was built in 1960. It's still one of the more affordable courses in the area, as well as one of the more chal-

Lake Tahoe Golf Course.

lenging thanks to extremely narrow fairways hemmed in by walls of pine trees. It's short—just 4028 yards, 66 par. Handcart, electric cart and club rentals are available, as well as lessons, and there's a driving range and putting green. Open April through November. ~ 3021 Route 50; 530-577-2121; www.tahoeparadisegolf.com.

For spectacular scenery, few courses can compare with the California State Parks and Recreation Department's 18-hole **Lake Tahoe Golf Course**, a 6707-yard, par-71 green. Built along a scenic stretch of the Upper Truckee River (talk about water hazards!), it's punctuated with a wide variety of natural vegetation and has views of high granite ridges that keep their snow caps through most of the season. Club and cart rentals are available. Open April through October; reservations are taken up to 60 days in advance. ~ 2500 Route 50; 530-577-0788.

FISHING

The fishing season lasts all year at Lake Tahoe, and you can fish with either a California or Nevada fishing license regardless of which shore you're standing on. Both the California Department of Fish and Game (916-355-0978; www.dfg.ca.gov) and the Nevada Division of Wildlife (775-

How about a Big Mack?

Lake Tahoe is so famous for its Mackinaw trout that just about every angler who comes to the lake dreams of landing one. Also called lake trout, these giants can weigh in at close to 40 pounds and measure longer than your arm. They swim in cold and darkness at depths of 200 to 300 feet, so sonar is required to locate them, and special tackle—including at least 1200 feet of fishing line—is required to land one. This generally means hiring a sportfishing charter operator. Catch-and-release fishing is strongly encouraged to avoid depleting the number and size of Lake Tahoe's Mackinaws, which can live more than 40 years. A fishing guide can show you how to deflate the fish, which puffs up from the change in water pressure when it is drawn to the surface from a great depth, then safely unhook it, photograph it, and throw it back to continue its career as a temporary trophy.

688-1500) stock the lake regularly with rainbow trout and intermittently with eastern brook trout and kokanee salmon. Because of the water's depth and the lake's sheer size, chances are slim to none of catching these trout from a boat, so most fishing is done from shore—with one exception. Sportfishing charter boats equipped with deepwater sonar offer anglers a chance to try for the giant Mackinaw trout that live at depths of 200 feet or more beneath the water. Although not required, charter operators strongly encourage catch-and-release fishing.

JUST FOR KIDS: TROUT FISHING MADE SIMPLE

Families with small children may wish to try their luck at the **Tahoe Trout Farm**. It's kind of like shooting fish in a barrel; the operators of this private enterprise stock their pond just as fast as you can pull the fish out. It's also kind of like buying fish at the supermarket because you pay by the fish for your catch. Bait and tackle are free. Open Memorial Day through Labor Day. Admission. ~ 1023 Blue Lake Avenue, South Lake Tahoe; 530-541-1491.

In South Lake Tahoe, contact any of the numerous deep-water sportfishing charter operators for Mackinaw safaris. They include: **Don Sheetz Guide Service** (530-541-5566, 877-270-0742), **Rick Muller's Sport Fishing** (530-544-4358), **Tahoe Sportfishing** (Tahoe Keys Marina, 900 Ski Run Boulevard; 530-696-7797; www.tahoesports.com, e-mail gofish@tahoesports.com), **Sierra Sportfishing** (Tahoe Keys Marina, 900 Ski Run Boulevard; 530-544-0229; www.sierrasportfishing.com) and **Mile High Fishing Charters** (530-541-5312; www.fishtahoe.com, e-mail milehighfishing@aol.com).

Fishing in the big lake is not the only game in town. Many of the lakes to the south in Eldorado National Forest offer good bait fishing. A favorite in the South Lake Tahoe area is **Echo Lakes**, where big rainbow trout are abundant and anglers also hook brook trout, cutthroat trout and kokanee salmon. ~ Echo Chalet; 530-659-7207.

For flyfishing equipment and rentals, advice on the most productive flyfishing streams, and guide service, contact **Tahoe Fly Fishing Outfitters**. ~ 3433 Lake Tahoe Boulevard; 530-541-8208.

Castle
East About

BALLOON RIDES

Three-hour hot-air balloon flights that start at dawn with a trip above the mountains before heading out across the lake, landing on the deck of a 40-foot boat for a champagne cruise back to shore, are offered by **Balloons Over Lake Tahoe**. Reservations are required. ~ 530-544-7008; www.balloonsoverlaketahoe.com. **Lake Tahoe Balloons** offers dawn balloon excursions that both take off and land from a boat deck and operate year-round, weather permitting. ~ 530-544-1221, 800-872-9294.

WINTER SPORTS

The overwhelming South Shore presence in wintertime is **Heavenly Lake Tahoe**, bigger and more complicated than any other downhill ski area in the region, with a gondola, an aerial tram, a six-passenger chairlift, five high-speed four-passenger lifts, eight three-passenger lifts, five doubles and seven surface lifts. The 4800 acres of ski slopes have 82 runs, almost half of them rated intermediate, some more than five miles long. The maximum vertical drop is 3500 feet from a maximum elevation of 10,040 feet. The views across the lake and the High Sierra are as exciting as the runs themselves. There's no way to ski all the bowls, ridges and trails—or even just the beginner and intermediate ones—in a single visit. Snowboarding is allowed everywhere in the ski area, and there's also a large snowboard park with special features such as rolls, flattops and a half-pipe. Various state-of-the-art ski rental packages are available. Expect crowds. ~ 775-586-7000, 800-243-2836; www.skiheavenly.com.

A somewhat smaller and much quieter ski area, **Sierra-at-Tahoe** offers not only the best beginners' runs around, such as the 2.5-mile Sugar'n'Spice, but also roller-coaster intermediate trails through the woods and a great view from the barbecue restaurant at the summit. Sierra-at-Tahoe has 2000 acres of skiable terrain with 46 runs and a max-

OPPOSITE: Sierra-at-Tahoe.

imum vertical drop of 2212 feet from an 8852-foot summit. Snowboarding is allowed, and there's an exceptional snowboard park. You have a choice of standard and high-performance ski rental packages. The ski area is located 13 miles west of town off Route 150, and free shuttles run regularly from all major Stateline and South Lake Tahoe hotels. ~ 1111 Sierra at Tahoe Road, Twin Bridges; 530-659-7453, snow conditions 530-659-7475; www.sierratahoe.com, e-mail sierra@sierra.com.

SLIP AND SLIDE

For those burned out on skiing and seeking other forms of winter jollies, South Lake Tahoe's Parks & Recreation Department operates an **Ice Arena** for skating on a regulation hockey-size indoor rink, just across the street from El Dorado Beach, year-round. ~ 1176 Rufus Allen Boulevard; 530-542-6262. There's a tube and saucer sled hill at **Hansen's Resort**, near the foot of Heavenly Lake Tahoe. Equipment is provided, and you can warm up in the resort's redwood hot tub. ~ 1360 Ski Run Boulevard; 530-544-3361.

The huge Heavenly Lake Tahoe downhill ski area recently opened **Heavenly's Mountain Adventure Center**, probably the smallest Nordic ski area on the lake as well as the most perfectly groomed. Its 2.5 kilometers of cross-country and snowshoeing trails even have passing lanes. Ski rentals are available. ~ Heavenly Lake Tahoe, South Lake Tahoe; 775-586-7000.

You'll find another 4 kilometers of well-groomed trails at **Lake Tahoe Winter Sports Center**, along the Truckee River. There are another 18 kilometers of ungroomed, ski-packed trails. Rentals available. ~ Route 50, Myers; 530-577-2940.

Cross-country skiing is also allowed on the snow-packed trails of **Bijou Community Park**, right in the center of South Lake Tahoe. ~ Tahoe Boulevard at Johnson Boulevard; 530-542-6056.

For more challenging cross-country skiing in the forested mountains along the Tahoe Rim, take the **Echo Lakes Trail** from Johnson Pass south of South Lake Tahoe. It's 4 kilometers around the shoreline to the northwest corner of Upper Echo Lake. From there the trail continues another six kilometers up strenuous terrain to Lake Aloha, a water wonderland few people see in winter. A Sno-park is required to park your car near the trailhead in winter.

CAMPING

Right in the middle of downtown South Lake Tahoe, the municipal **Campground by the Lake** is within walking distance of just about everything and offers more ambience than you'd expect, with shady evergreens sheltering the 170 tent/RV sites. There's drinking water, a dump station, and restrooms with showers. Pet owners must show a certificate of rabies vaccination. Sites cost $21.50 to $29.50 per night. Open April through October. ~ 1150 Rufus Allen Boulevard; 530-542-6096; www.ci.south-lake-tahoe.ca.us.

When it comes to private campgrounds, the biggest and best in town is **Tahoe Valley**. It has 112 tent and 301 RV sites with full hookups including cable TV. Facilities include not only restrooms, showers and a dump station but also a swimming pool, tennis courts and even a concierge. Sites cost $24 to $42 per night. ~ 1175 Melba Drive; 530-541-2222.

Less than idyllic but ideally located, the **Lakeside RV Park** is adjacent to Lakeside Marina, with its boat and water ski rentals, and within easy walking distance of the Stateline casino resorts. Its 43 RV sites have full hookups including TV cables. Sites cost $30 per night. ~ 3987 Cedar Avenue; 530-544-4704; www.tahoerv.com.

True Romance: Lake Tahoe's Wedding Industry

Lake Tahoe is one of the most popular places on the West Coast for couples to take their marriage vows. Neither California nor Nevada has a waiting period or blood test requirement. With more than 50 wedding chapels around the lake, you can be married in a casino or a gourmet restaurant. You can also tie the knot in a hot-air balloon, on a mountaintop or in picturesque Vikingsholm Castle. You can be wed by a cruise ship captain in the middle of the lake. But perhaps no place in Tahoe is more wedding-minded than the **Fantasy Inn & Wedding Chapel**, with its 15 fantasy-themed rooms and suites. Choose among the Tropical Treehouse, the Arabian Nights room, the Antony and Cleopatra room, the Romeo and Juliet suite, the Graceland suite and others. Various rooms have heart-shaped whirlpool baths, two-person showers, fireplaces, round king-size beds and lots of mirrors. ~ 3696 Lake Tahoe Boulevard, South Lake Tahoe; 530-541-4200, 800-367-7763; www.fantasy-inn.com, e-mail info@fantasy-inn.com. ULTRA-DELUXE.

lodging

In operation since 1965, the **Christiania Inn** has a breathtaking location at the base of the main Heavenly chairlift. A European alpine feel permeates this classic country lodge with six guest rooms and suites. Each room has a king- or queen-size brass or pedestal bed and Victorian-style furnishings. Most have woodburning fireplaces, and some have saunas or whirlpool tubs, as well as views of Heavenly's legendary Gunbarrel ski run. Surrounded by pines, "the Chris" is also one of South Lake Tahoe's premier fine-dining establishments. ~ 3819 Saddle Road; 530-544-7337, fax 530-544-5342; www.christianiainn.com; e-mail thechris@sierra.net. MODERATE TO DELUXE.

Near the base of Heavenly Lake Tahoe, **Hansen's Resort** rents semi-secluded cabins in the woods as well as pine-paneled, spotlessly clean motel-style rooms—all within walking distance of the Heavenly Gondola, the Stateline casino resorts, several marinas and the shops, galleries and restaurants of downtown South Lake Tahoe. ~ 1360 Ski Run Boulevard; 530-544-3361, fax 530-543-0702. MODERATE TO DELUXE.

In the same area, you'll find 14 elegant, individually decorated suites and cabins at the **Inn at Heavenly**. All of the spa-

Hansen's Resort.

cious units have wood-plank ceilings and ceiling fans, refrigerators, microwaves, coffeemakers, laptop hookups and televisions with VCRs, and all have patchwork quilts and handmade furniture. Decor ranges from High Sierra rustic to Southwestern and chic contemporary styles. The inn is set in the middle of two shady, heavily wooded acres. Rates include a continental breakfast and evening wine and hors d'oeuvres, plus snacks available all day long. Each guest or couple gets the private use of the spa room, with its large hot tub, steam bath and sauna, for one hour a day. ~ 1261 Ski Run Boulevard; 530-544-4244, 800-692-2246, fax 530-544-5213; www.800my cabin.com. DELUXE TO ULTRA-DELUXE.

The neighboring **Black Bear Inn**, one of Lake Tahoe's most prestigious bed and breakfasts, also has a woodland setting. Each of the lodge rooms and cabins has a king-size bed and a river-rock fireplace and is beautifully decorated with an individualized blend of rustic and modern furnishings. The central living room features a massive floor-to-ceiling fireplace and a baby grand piano. The high-ceilinged cabins have kitchenettes; one has a private two-person jacuzzi. ~ 1202 Ski Run Boulevard; 530-544-4451, 877-232-7466; www.tahoeblack bear.com, e-mail info@tahoeblackbear.com. ULTRA-DELUXE.

A small motel-style lodging, **Seven Seas Inn at Tahoe** rents 17 guest rooms, some of them with gas fireplaces. The hot tub is great for soothing those muscles after a day of hiking or skiing. ~ 4145 Manzanita Avenue; 530-544-7031, 800-800-7327, fax 530-544-1208; www.sevenseastahoe.com, e-mail sevenseas@sprynet.com. BUDGET TO MODERATE.

Nearby, the **Blue Jay Lodge** offers reasonable rates on conventional rooms, as well as suites with kitchens and fireplaces—all a block from the Stateline casinos. Facilities include a heated pool and a spa. ~ 4133 Cedar Avenue; 530-544-5232, 800-258-3529, fax 530-544-0453; www.bluejaylodge.com, e-mail jc@bluejaylodge.com. BUDGET TO MODERATE.

A classy motor inn with a ski-lodge look and a wide range of room options, the 100-unit **Inn by the Lake** sits on landscaped grounds well back from the highway. Many of the pretty pastel rooms have lake views, and the suites have full kitchens.

Facilities include a swimming pool, a sauna and a split-level hot tub. ~ 3300 Lake Tahoe Boulevard; 530-542-0330, 800-877-1466, fax 530-541-6596; www.innbythelake.com, e-mail info@innbythelake.com. MODERATE TO ULTRA-DELUXE.

Yes, you can find affordable accommodations at Lake Tahoe. **Sky Lake Lodge**, on the South Shore's main commercial thoroughfare, has 23 guest rooms decorated with a certain panache that sets them apart from the usual "standard" motel room. Each room has two double beds or one queen-size bed, telephone, television and enclosed shower. ~ 2644 Lake Tahoe Boulevard; 530-544-0770. BUDGET.

dining

The **Christiania Inn** serves fare that includes appetizers like beluga caviar and salmon carpaccio, followed by entrées such as rack of lamb, a fresh seafood platter or a selection from a Continental cuisine menu that changes seasonally, all flawlessly prepared by graduates of the Culinary Institute. Couple this with a crackling fire in the fireplace and your choice from one of the largest wine cellars in the Lake Tahoe area. Live music on weekends. Closed Monday in spring and summer. ~ 3819 Saddle Road; 530-544-7337, fax 530-544-5342; www.christianiainn.com, e-mail thechris@sierra.net. DELUXE.

The setting is half the fun at **Fresh Ketch**, the restaurant at Tahoe Keys Marina with indoor and outdoor seating and a view of the yacht basin. As you'd expect, seafood is the focus, from clam chowder and oysters to Alaskan king crab claws and Baja-style fish tacos. Of special note is the selection of beers, including imports from around the world as well as California microbrews. ~ 2435 Venice Drive; 530-541-5683. MODERATE TO DELUXE.

For Thai food at Lake Tahoe, the place to go is the **Siam Restaurant**, a casual place with unpretentious booth seating and a menu that covers a wide range of dishes such as squid, red snapper, spicy roast duck and, of course, assorted coconut-milk curry dishes. A local favorite. Closed Tuesday. ~ 2180 Lake Tahoe Boulevard; 530-544-0370; e-mail watrj8164@aol.com.

The Dory's Oar strives, with considerable success, to foster a Maine coast atmosphere on the shore of Lake Tahoe. Housed in a red New England—style cottage with green shutters, the restaurant has a menu to match: Eastern clams and oysters, Chesapeake Bay softshelled crabs and stuffed baby salmon. You can pick out a live Maine lobster from a display tank and have it cooked to order. Upstairs, the **Tudor Pub** serves traditional pub grub such as shepherd's pie and fish-and-chips. ~ 1041 Fremont Avenue; 530-541-6603; www.dorysoar.com, e-mail dorysoar@aol.com. MODERATE TO DELUXE.

An intimate little Lake Tahoe original, **Evan's American Gourmet Café** is tucked away in a little cottage just past the "Y" on the way to the West Shore. With only 11 tables, the service is attentive, and the ambience, with its soft lighting, original artwork and soft earth-and-water hues, sets the stage for outstanding cuisine. While the menu varies according to the availability of fresh ingredients, dinner here might start with an appetizer such as wild mushroom phyllo pastry, followed by a main course of venison with balsamic cherries and fresh tarragon. The homemade desserts are extra-special. Dinner only. ~ 536 Emerald Bay Road; 530-542-1990, fax 530-542-9111; www.evanstahoe.com. DELUXE.

BREAKFAST FOR CHAMPS

If your stomach is craving attention, **Frank's Restaurant**. Serving breakfast until 2 p.m., along with a standard selection of light lunch choices, Frank's claim to fame is the biggest breakfast menu in town. The 200-plus selections include more than 30 kinds of omelettes as well as breakfast burritos, crêpes, fruit waffles and just about any other eye-opening meal you can think of. ~ 1207 Route 50; 530-544-3434. BUDGET.

The same folks that own Evan's also run **The Cantina**, a gourmet establishment with a whole different flavor—Southwest nouveau. In addition to standard border fare like enchiladas, fajitas and green chile, you'll find Santa Fe–style dishes such as blue corn–crusted salmon and Tex-Mex crab cakes, as well as a long list of daily specials. ~ 765 Emerald Bay Road; 530-544-1233; www.cantinatahoe.com. MODERATE.

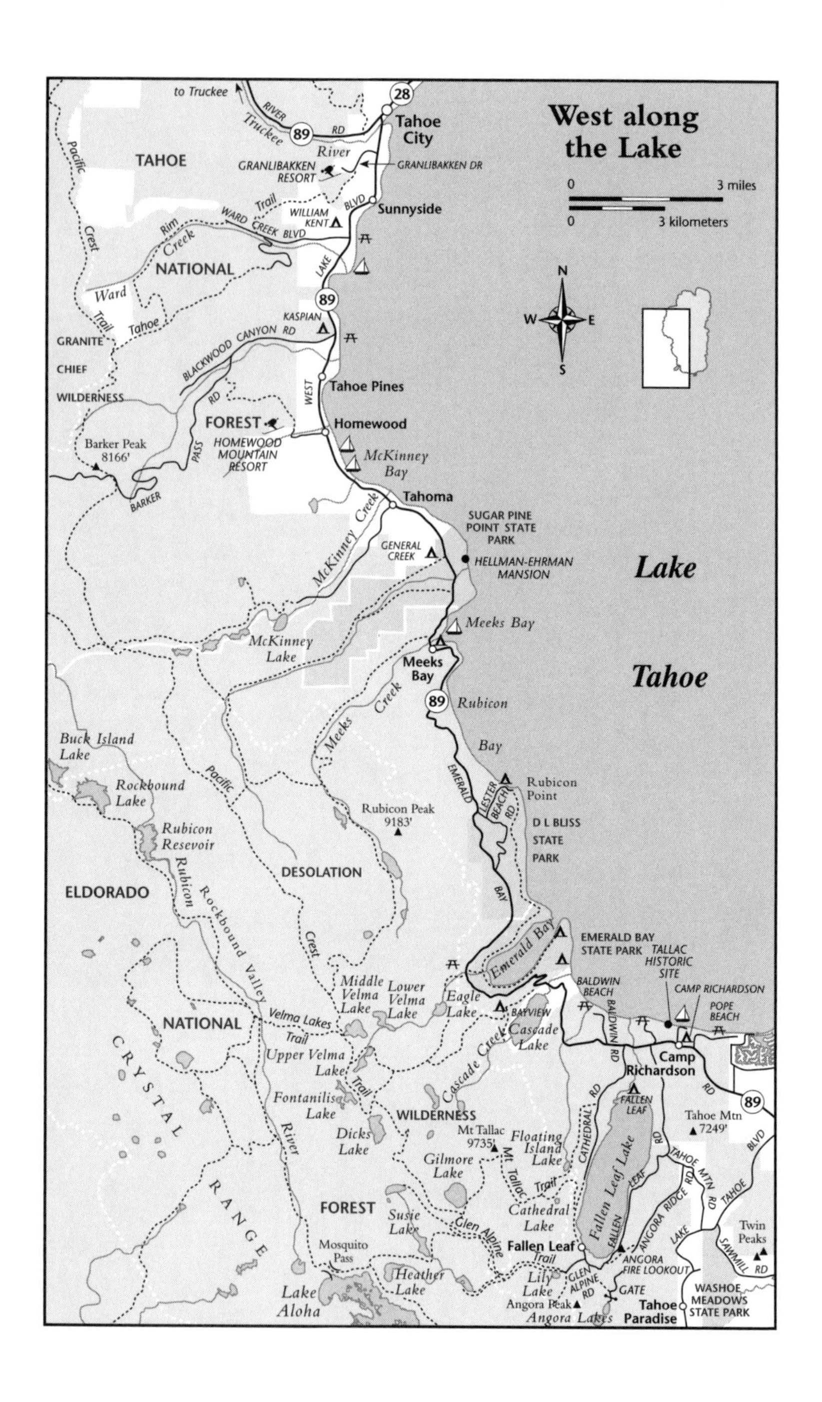

West along the Lake
0
3 miles
0
3 kilometers
N
W
E
S
to Truckee
28
Tahoe City
Truckee River Rd
89
River
TAHOE
GRANLIBAKKEN RESORT
GRANLIBAKKEN DR
Pacific Crest Trail
Trail
WILLIAM KENT
BLVD
Sunnyside
Rim
WARD CREEK BLVD
Creek
NATIONAL
Ward
LAKE
Trail
Tahoe
89
KASPIAN
GRANITE CHIEF WILDERNESS
BLACKWOOD CANYON RD
Tahoe Pines
WEST
FOREST
Homewood
HOMEWOOD MOUNTAIN RESORT
Barker Peak 8166'
PASS
BARKER
McKinney Bay
Tahoma
McKinney Creek
SUGAR PINE POINT STATE PARK
GENERAL CREEK
HELLMAN-EHRMAN MANSION
Lake
Tahoe
Meeks Bay
McKinney Lake
Meeks Bay
89
Rubicon Bay
Meeks Creek
Buck Island Lake
Rockbound Lake
Pacific
EMERALD
LESTER BEACH RD
Rubicon Point
Rubicon Peak 9183'
D L BLISS STATE PARK
Rubicon Reservoir
Rubicon
Rockbound Valley
DESOLATION
ELDORADO
BAY
Crest
Emerald Bay
EMERALD BAY STATE PARK
TALLAC HISTORIC SITE
CAMP RICHARDSON
BALDWIN BEACH
POPE BEACH
Middle Velma Lake
Lower Velma Lake
Eagle Lake
BAYVIEW
BALDWIN RD
Velma Lakes Trail
NATIONAL
Cascade Creek
Cascade Lake
Camp Richardson
Upper Velma Lake
CRYSTAL RANGE
RD
89
FALLEN LEAF
Trail
Fontanilis Lake
WILDERNESS
CATHEDRAL RD
Tahoe Mtn 7249'
River
Dicks Lake
Mt Tallac 9735'
Floating Island Lake
Fallen Leaf Lake
RD
BLVD
Mt Tallac Trail
TAHOE MTN RD
Gilmore Lake
LEAF
TAHOE
FOREST
Cathedral Lake
ANGORA RIDGE RD
Susie Lake
Glen Alpine
FALLEN
LAKE
Twin Peaks
Mosquito Pass
Fallen Leaf
Trail
ANGORA FIRE LOOKOUT
SAWMILL RD
Heather Lake
Lily Lake
GLEN ALPINE RD
GATE
WASHOE MEADOWS STATE PARK
Lake Aloha
Angora Peak
Tahoe Paradise
Angora Lakes

7

West along the Lake

The 28 miles of road along Lake Tahoe's West Shore from South Lake Tahoe to Tahoe City has been called "the most beautiful drive in America." Of course, the visitors bureau copywriters who came up with that slogan may have a penchant for hyperbole; either that or they've never driven Yosemite's Tioga Road or the California Coast's Highway 1. But it's probably fair to rank this scenic route along the wild side of the lake as one of the top ten.

More than any other part of the lake, the West Shore has a national park feel, with its undeveloped shorelines, pristine forest, waterfalls and astonishing vistas overlooking picturesque bays and coves. Equally fascinating are the magnificent Vikingsholm Castle and other mansions left behind by the wealthy folks who built their ostentatious vacation homes along Lake Tahoe's shore in the early 20th century. This is the kind of drive that, once you've completed it, makes you want to turn around and do it all over again.

sightseeing

Driving west (away from Stateline) in South Lake Tahoe, you'll come to the "Y" at the edge of town, at a stoplight beside a shopping center and large office supply store. Turn right on Emerald Bay Road (Route 89 North) and you're on your way up the west shore of the lake.

On your right, sandy **Pope Beach** extends between the lake and a fringe of evergreens, a more pleasant beach than any in South Lake Tahoe itself and, because of its proximity to Historic Camp Richardson Resort, one of the most popular beaches on the lake. There are restrooms, picnic tables and barbecue grills, and the gradual slope of the beach makes it a good place for swimming. The public parking area charges $3 per vehicle and fills up fast on warm summer days. You can avoid the fee and the parking hassle by taking the trolley from South Lake Tahoe or getting to the beach by bike. No dogs are allowed on this or any other beach on the California side of Lake Tahoe. ~ Lake Tahoe Basin Management Unit, 530-573-2600.

Just past Pope Beach, **Historic Camp Richardson Resort** is a sprawling complex of lodging, camping and recreational facilities that has been around since 1921. Although a latecomer among the grand old resorts that graced the South Shore, it's the last one standing. Entrepreneur Alonzo

Richardson, who started a tour company to bring visitors to Lake Tahoe by automobile, built a cluster of lakefront cabins on the site, naming each one after a motor vehicle. A few years later, when neighboring Tallac Resort burned down, he salvaged materials from the remaining buildings to erect a central lodge. As Camp Richardson sprawled into a huge resort complex over the years, it retained its classic 1920s woodframe architecture and still has an old-time look. ~ Emerald Bay Road; 530-541-1801, 800-544-1801, fax 530-541-1802; www.camprichardson.com.

Just past Camp Richardson, a concrete foundation at **Tallac Historic Site** is all that remains of the elegant Tallac Resort, which was built in 1873. It boasted croquet and tennis courts, bowling alleys, a theater and a ballroom that could accommodate 250 guests, as well as the first electric lights on the lakefront, and became known as the "Greatest Casino in America," but deteriorated as Lake Tahoe's upper-crust exclusivity gave way to a more egalitarian brand of tourism. Sadly, it was demolished in 1920 after a bout of deterioration. Visitors can stroll along the tree-sheltered lawn that meets the shoreline. Rangers conduct guided tours daily. Open Memorial Day to Labor Day. ~ Emerald Bay Road; 530-541-5227.

Recalling Bygone Days

The Pope Estate at Tallac Historic Site hosts the annual **Great Gatsby Festival** on the second weekend in August. The two-day event takes you back to 1920s high-society life with a living history program and costumed actors who provide tours. There are vintage vendors, antique cars, food, live music and children's activities. All activities are free or inexpensive except the Sunday afternoon tea and fashion show, which costs $25. Reservations are required. ~ 530-544-7383.

Other **living history programs** are held at Tallac Historic Site throughout the summer. Among them are children's activities including garden parties, a 1920s school class and a chance to cook in an old-fashioned kitchen. Adults can have high tea amid the exotic plants and reflecting pool of the Pope Arboretum. There is a fee for most activities, and reservations are required.

On the last weekend in July at the Heller Estate, the Washoe Tribe of California and Nevada presents the annual **Wa She Shu it Deh Native American Arts Festival** with craft demonstrations, storytelling, music and dance, and food booths.

Over the Rainbow and through the Woods

The Taylor Creek Visitors Center has several trails that provide a glimpse of some of the area's treasures. The half-mile **Rainbow Trail** loop takes visitors along a boardwalk and over bridges, through the forest, meadow and marsh near the mouth of Taylor Creek, a good place to watch birds and small mammals—and to fish. Along the trail, the Stream Profile Chamber lets you view Taylor Creek both above and below the water's surface through floor-to-ceiling bay windows and observe the fish in their natural environment. The longest of the visitors center nature trails, the **Lake of the Sky Trail** goes from the visitors center to the lakefront, then east along the shore to the historic estates of Tallac Historic Site. Return from the Tallac parking area to the visitors center on the **Tallac Historic Site Trail** for a two-mile loop trip.

Three large estate homes still stand alongside the old Tallac property and have been restored as part of the historic site. Walking east from the parking area and hotel site, the first of the homes you reach is the Baldwin Estate, a giant log house built in 1921 by the heiress to the fortune amassed by the Tallac Resort's owners. It now houses the **Baldwin Museum**, with historic photographs of the hotel, the casino, and the lifestyle of the rich and famous at the early Lake Tahoe resorts, as well as exhibits on the Washoe Indians, Baldwin family and women of Tallac and Lake Tahoe. Open mid-June through September; closed Monday. Admission. ~ 530-541-5227.

The Pope Estate, the largest turn-of-the-20th-century estate on Lake Tahoe and the oldest (1894), was the summer home of a prominent San Francisco family. Its vast interiors and elaborate decor earned it the nickname "Vatican Lodge." Now undergoing restoration, the house can be seen on one of the guided tours offered on Tuesday, Friday and Saturday, by reservation only. Visitors can also tour the gardens and ground, as well as the estate boathouse, where you can see the restored

1921 cruiser *Quic-Chadkidn* (get it?), a 41-foot vessel formerly used to take cruises on the lake. Admission. ~ Reservations: 530-541-5227.

The showiest estate on Lake Tahoe is the Tallac Historic Site's **Heller Estate**, the former summer home of San Francisco financier Walter Heller, built in 1923. It is usually known by its nickname, "Valhalla." Although the estate is not open for tours, the Tahoe Tallac Association sponsors music concerts and arts-and-crafts events there throughout the summer. ~ 530-542-4166, 888-632-5859; www.valhalla-tallac.com.

Continuing a short distance west on Emerald Bay Road, you come to the U.S. Forest Service's **Taylor Creek Visitors Center**, where books, maps and trail brochures are available and rangers provide advice on hiking, biking and camping possibilities in the national forest. Most of the center's activities and points of interest are outdoors along several easy, wheelchair-accessible nature trails. The shortest are two interpretive loops, each less than a quarter-mile long, designed with young children in mind. The **Forest Tree Trail** has signs that tell the story of the Jeffrey pine, the most common evergreen in the Lake Tahoe area. The **Smokey Trail** presents tips on forest fire prevention and campfire safety. Open daily late May through

Baldwin Beach.

The Queen of Vikingsholm Castle

Lora Josephine Knight, who built Vikingsholm on Emerald Bay, was the daughter of a corporation attorney in small-town Illinois who became involved with railroad development during the "Robber Baron" era. Brilliant and ruthless, he amassed a fortune in corporate holdings. By the time Lora and her sisters inherited his estate, it included controlling interests in Nabisco, Continental Can, the Diamond Match Company and the Union Pacific and Rock Island railroads.

After burying her first husband and divorcing her second, Lora Knight bought 239 acres at the head of Emerald Bay, along with Fannette Island in the middle of the bay, where she built a private teahouse. She commissioned her niece's husband, Swedish architect Lennart Palme, to build Vikingsholm in medieval Scandinavian style as befit the fjordlike setting she had chosen. Mrs. Knight and the Palme family spent the summer of 1928 in Denmark, Finland, Norway and Sweden, visiting 11th-century Norse churches and Swedish castles and photographing them so that Palme could faithfully reproduce specific features at Vikingsholm.

Palme employed more than 200 workman to build Vikingsholm Castle, with its massive hand-hewn timbers, stone ramparts, intricately carved doors and roof ridges with dragon heads, in a single summer. Mrs. Knight continued to travel in Scandinavia, shopping for period antiques with which to furnish the castle. Many of the pieces she coveted were either in museum collections or so valuable that the governments of Sweden and Norway would not permit them to be exported, so she hired craftsmen to make exact reproductions of the pieces, even to the aging of the wood and the scratches on the originals. Lora Knight lived in the castle for 15 summers, until her death in 1945. Now owned by the California Parks Department, Vikingsholm is generally considered the finest example of medieval Scandinavian architecture in the United States.

September, open weekends only through October. ~ Lake Tahoe Basin Management Unit, 530-573-2674; www.r5.fs.fed.us/ltbmu.

West of Taylor Creek, the white-sand **Baldwin Beach** runs for a mile toward Eagle Point on the south shore of Emerald Bay. Facilities include picnic tables, barbecue grills and restrooms. Swimming is permitted, but no dogs are allowed. Parking fee, $3.

Continue on Emerald Bay Road, and on your left you'll pass the large, privately owned **Cascade Lake**, with a walking path around its east shore to Cascade Falls. As picturesque as it is accessible, the lake has been a frequent moviemaking location since the 1930s, when Nelson Eddy crooned to Jeanette MacDonald there.

Vikingsholm Castle.

As Cascade Lake fades from view, the road climbs onto a high, rocky ridge overlooking **Emerald Bay State Park** on your right—probably the most beautiful spot on the Lake Tahoe shore. The main road goes almost all the way around the narrow, fjordlike cove along steep, pine-robed slopes that rise 500 feet above the placid, blue-green water; little Fannette Island, Lake Tahoe's only island, sits solitary in the bay's center. Below a parking area at the west end of the bay tumbles spectacular **Eagle Falls**, the only waterfall that drops directly into Lake Tahoe. The park has picnic areas, restrooms, campgrounds and a road that winds down to the shore. Day-use fee.

The unique sight that sets Emerald Bay apart from other breathtaking views is **Vikingsholm Castle**, modeled after medieval Scandinavian fortresses and built in 1929. Daily tours of the 38-room stone castle, reached by walking down a steep old road, are offered for a fee from Memorial Day weekend through Labor Day weekend. ~ 530-525-7232.

Just up the road at **D.L. Bliss State Park**, you can stand on Rubicon Point and gaze down into the crystal-clear water to depths of more than 100 feet. Named after the area's lumber and railroad tycoon who once owned it, the 744-acre park has picnic areas, restrooms and hiking trails. Its most striking feature is **Balancing Rock**, a 130-ton granite boulder perched precariously alongside the half-mile nature trail in the northwest part of the park. Day-use fee. ~ 530-525-7277.

The shore of **Meeks Bay** is partly under private ownership and partly managed by the forest service. While marinas, private docks and vacation homes may be the most noticeable features of the bayshore, there is an attractive little white-sand public beach with picnic tables, fire pits and restrooms toward the north end. The adjacent resort beach operated by the Meeks

View from Rubicon Trail in D.L. Bliss State Park.

Bay Marina has paddleboats and assorted other water toys for rent. Parking fee, $3. ~ Lake Tahoe Basin Management Unit, 530-573-2674; Meeks Bay Marina, 530-525-5588.

Although it has the look of old-growth forest, the biggest of the East Shore's evergreen trees were cut down 80 to 120 years ago to build the historic resorts and mansions along the lake shore. One of the few places along the lakeshore where you can see truly virgin forest in its natural state is **Sugar Pine Point State Park**, just north of Meeks Bay. This magnificent 2000-acre woodland park spans almost two miles of shoreline and runs nearly four miles inland along General Creek. The land was originally the estate of financier Issias W. Hellman, who built a grand Queen Anne Victorian—style summer home called Pine Lodge there in 1903. Today the lodge is preserved as the **Hellman-Ehrman Mansion**, a museum dedicated to the lifestyle of the rich and famous at turn-of-the-20th-century Lake Tahoe. Nearby are an old pioneer cabin and a new nature center with live specimens of several species of birds, mammals and fish that live in the Lake Tahoe Basin, as well as exhibits about lake ecology, wildflowers and trees. Park facilities include picnic areas, restrooms and tennis courts. The park is open year-round, but the museum is only open July through Labor Day. ~ 530-525-7982.

Just beyond Sugar Pine Point State Park, the road begins its return to civilization in **Tahoma**, a vacation home community with a population of 500, making it the largest town on the West Shore. The last ten miles of the drive to Tahoe City also take you through **Homewood**, a tiny ski village.

outdoor adventures

HIKING

The forested slopes that rise across the road from the lakeshore have few trailheads to hint at what may lie beyond the nearest ridgeline. In fact, along much of the West

Shore, the boundary of the vast, roadless Desolation Wilderness with its profusion of alpine lakes and crags of bare granite approaches within as little as a quarter-mile of the Lake Tahoe, though getting to it may require a roundabout all-day or longer trek. The Pacific Crest and Tahoe Rim Trail, the main route through the wilderness, goes 32.5 miles between trailheads. For the less adventurous, the West Shore also offers a number of day-hikes, from mellow lakeshore walks to an ambitious climb up a mountain overlooking the lake. Distances listed for all trails are one way unless otherwise noted.

For a gentle hike in the Camp Richardson area, besides the sightseeing trails mentioned earlier at Tallac Historic Site and the Taylor Creek Visitors Center, there's the 1-mile **Angora Lakes Trail**. To reach the trailhead, from Fallen Leaf Campground across the road from Tallac Historic Site, take Fallen Leaf Road south for two miles, turn left on Tahoe Mountain Road, and then take the next right onto unpaved Angora Ridge

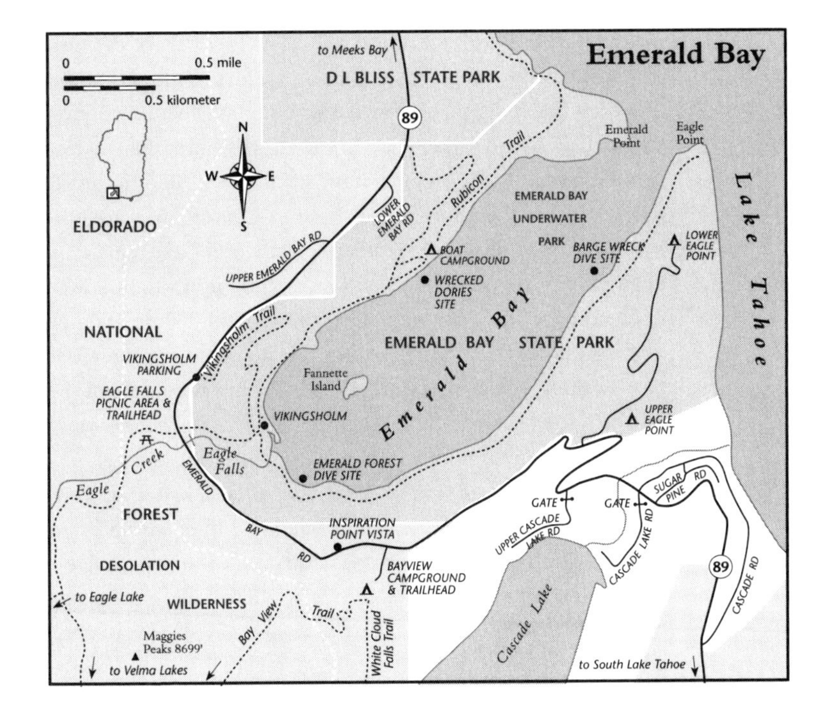

Road (Forest Road 1214). Drive three miles to the parking area and trailhead. Partway up the road, the old Angora Fire Lookout offers a view of Fallen Leaf Lake and the Camp Richardson area from 500 feet above. Once you're on the wide trail, it's a mile upgrade around the wooded shore of Lower Angora Lake, ending as it reaches Upper Angora Lake, a picture-perfect spot with the dark cliffs of Angora Peak and Echo Peak, marking the Desolation Wilderness boundary, as a backdrop. The lake is a locally popular area where families with small kids and dogs go on weekends. There's a swimming beach, a rowboat rental dock and a snack bar.

SUNKEN PLEASURE

Found along Mount Tallac Trail, **Floating Island Lake** is a small, buggy, not-too-appealing pond that's interesting mostly because of its history. In the late 19th century, there actually was a floating island of shrubbery with a single sizeable tree in the lake. Vintage photos show old-time resort guests paddling the island around the lake. It eventually sank.

Not all hikes in this area are so easy. The 5-mile **Mount Tallac Trail** takes hikers all the way to the mountain's summit with a 3250-foot elevation gain. The first part of the trail switchbacks up a sagebrush slope. It then runs along the top of a ridgeline and up and down a series of hills before coming to Floating Island Lake. Past this point, you enter the Desolation Wilderness so you must have a wilderness permit, available for free at the Taylor Creek Visitors Center; bikes are prohibited. A short distance farther on, Cathedral Lake marks the beginning of the very steep two-mile climb up the south face of Mount Tallac. (The north side, toward Lake Tahoe, is twice as steep and virtually unclimbable.) If you make it to the 9735-foot summit, you'll be rewarded with a panoramic view of the lake and the peaks of the Desolation Wilderness that's simply breathtaking (assuming you have any breath left to take).

If you continued on the same trail after descending from the Mount Tallac summit, about one more mile would bring you to Gilmore Lake, where you could join the Pacific Crest and Tahoe Rim Trail and continue south to Lake Aloha (see "Hiking" in Chapter 6). There's a shorter route, however, which doesn't require climbing a mountain to get there. To hike the 6-mile **Glen Alpine Trail**, first drive south from Historic Camp Richardson on Fallen Leaf Road, which hugs the east shore of Fallen Leaf Lake. The parking area and trailhead is about half a mile past the marina at the south end of the lake. The first three miles of the trail follow a creek steadily—and sometimes steeply—upward until it passes through a notch, joins the Pacific Crest and Tahoe Rim Trail and eases down to the shore of pretty Susie Lake. Another three-quarters of a mile brings you around the lakeshore and through a cut in the dramatic granite walls that surround Heather Lake. From there, it's just a short hike to big Lake Aloha, with its amazing setting at the head of Desolation Valley, surrounded by sheer cliffs over a thousand feet high in places and filled with little granite islands. When you reach the shore, you can turn right or left and walk the length of the lake; if you go right, you can continue climbing to Mosquito Pass—or at least partway up—for a great view of the entire lake. A wilderness permit, available at the Taylor Creek Visitors Center, is required for this hike; bikes are prohibited.

A short, varied and scenic hike from Bayview Campground above Emerald Bay, the 1-mile **White Cloud Falls Trail** starts near the campground's information kiosk and ascends gradually through tall pine forest to a stairway that climbs to a vista point overlooking Cascade Lake, White Cloud Falls and Lake Tahoe. Beyond, the trail makes an equally gradual descent above Cascade Lake, edging along the base of a granite cliff and crossing a talus field to the falls.

Another short hike above Emerald Bay, but a more strenuous one with a 400-foot elevation gain, the 1-mile **Eagle Falls Trail** to Eagle Lake starts at the parking area above the falls. Since the trail goes into the Desolation Wilderness, a wilderness permit is required, which only means you must fill out a form at the trailhead and drop it into a box there. You start by crossing a bridge over the falls, then climbing up a narrow defile along Eagle Creek on a series of granite stairways. As the terrain broadens, you get a view of Eagle Falls and Emerald Bay far below and soon reach Eagle Lake, a classic alpine lake within a fortress of gravel slopes and brooding cliffs. On any given summer day, a hundred or more visitors hike to the lake, but hardly any go farther. If you continue four more miles on the same trail, you'll reach the three clustered Velma Lakes—large, clear, dark, wooded and solitary. Beyond Middle Velma Lake, the trail fragments into four different routes heading off to different parts of the wilderness area. One trail that goes off to the left continues up to Fontanillis Lake and Dicks Lake, gaining another 400 feet in elevation. A short distance past the second lake, the trail splits. Take the left (downhill) fork, and you'll loop back to the trail you came up on. No bikes.

All three state parks along the West Shore offer exceptional day-hike opportunities. In Emerald Bay State Park, most visitors take the steep walkway (once a driveway) down to Vikingsholm by the water's edge, but relatively few continue on the **Rubicon Trail**, which goes 6.5 miles to D.L. Bliss State Park, where an early-20th-century lighthouse stands. No bikes.

In Sugar Pine Point State Park, the **General Creek Trail** makes a 2-mile loop as it takes you on a gentle tour through a lush, shadowy forest of 200-foot-tall trees up one side of the creek and back down the other with minimal climbing. If you're up for a longer hike, you can follow the

To experience the most scenic hike on the Lake Tahoe shoreline, take the **Rubicon Trail** from Vikingsholm in Emerald Bay State Park for two miles out to Emerald Point at the end of the bay's north shore, then another 4.5 miles to Rubicon Point in D.L. Bliss State Park.

Opposite: Rubicon Trail.

creek for another four, increasingly steep miles from the upper end of the loop, ending at a remote four-wheel-drive road without passing any notable landmarks along the way—just the sylvan beauty and silence of the Jeffrey and sugar pines. Because this trail doesn't actually go much of anywhere, you won't meet many other hikers on it.

BIKING

There are good, paved bike paths along much of the West Shore. One, which starts from Emerald Bay Road at the outskirts of South Lake Tahoe, follows the lakeshore for 6 miles past Pope Beach, Historic Camp Richardson, Tallac Historic Site and Baldwin Beach. It returns to the automobile road just before the steep climb up to the ridge overlooking Emerald Bay. If you want to make a complete tour of the West Shore by bike, you must use the bike lane at the side of the road from Emerald Bay to Meeks Bay, a distance of 12 miles. At Sugar Pine Point State Park, another bike path starts and parallels the road for 10 miles to Tahoe City.

Biking in Tallic Historic Site.

Because most West Shore trails of any length lead into the Desolation Wilderness, mountain biking is prohibited on them. The same is true of trails in the state parks. Serious mountain bikers may wish to tackle the 18.5-mile **McKinney-Rubicon Jeep Trail**, which follows McKinney Creek past a series of sunlit mountain lakes and crosses the Pacific Crest and Tahoe Rim trail on its way to Buck Island Lake and Rockbound Lake on the edge of the wilderness, then descends the west side of the Tahoe Rim to the Rubicon River.

Another four-wheel-drive road in the same area that bike enthusiasts favor is the rugged, narrow, sometimes steep old **Barker Pass Road**. To reach it, turn west at Kaspian Campground, two miles north of Homewood. After about three miles, the paved road turns sharply left to cross Blackwood Creek on a battered former dam, but an older road continues straight ahead through a gate on which a sign announces that it is a "special-use area" reserved for off-road vehicles— mountain bikes as well as high-clearance four-wheel-drive vehicles and ATVs. It's a steep, dusty 5-mile climb to the top of the pass, where the old road rejoins the new road at the Barker Pass trailhead for the Tahoe Rim Trail. (Bikes are not allowed on this section of the trail, which goes south into the Desolation Wilderness and north into the Granite Creek Wilderness, where wheeled vehicles are not allowed.) The thrill in this trip is the ride back down.

HAVE HORSE WILL TRAVEL

The **Camp Richardson Corral and Pack Station** has been taking visitors on scenic rides since 1934. They offer one- to two-hour trips through nearby meadows and forest as well as half-day trips to Floating Island Lake. In addition, they organize overnight and longer pack trips into the wilderness, and they will "spot pack" you and your gear into a back-country destination of your choice, help set up your camp and leave you there, returning with the horses on the day of your choice. The stable also offers timber wagon rides in summer and sleigh rides in winter. Reservations required for all rides. ~ Emerald Bay Road at Fallen Leaf Road; 530-541-3113, 877-541-3113.

HORSEBACK RIDING

Near Emerald Bay State Park, **Cascade Stables** has one-hour to half-day guided horseback tours to

Cascade Lake, as well as all-day and overnight trips to Velma Lakes or other destinations in the Desolation Wilderness. ~ Emerald Bay Road, Mile 6; 530-541-2055.

FISHING

Fallen Leaf Lake, the large lake a short distance inland from Tallac Historic Site, is stocked regularly with kokanee salmon. It also has smaller populations of rainbow trout and small, pan-size Mackinaw trout. The marina is located at the south end of this long, narrow lake.

Anglers who are willing to walk a ways for good fishing will find it in the alpine lakes of the **Desolation Wilderness** (see "Hiking" above). The California Department of Fish and Game seeds these lakes, dumping more than 120,000 young fish into them each year—by airplane. The catch can include not only the usual rainbow, brown and brook trout but also Mackinaws and golden trout. While dozens of lakes are likely candidates, those that come highly recommended by area fishing shops include Cathedral Lake, Heather Lake and Middle Velma Lake.

BOATING

Rental boats small and large, ranging from paddleboats, kayaks and Waverunners to big pontoon boats and ski craft, are available along Lake Tahoe's West Shore at Historic Camp Richardson's **Camp Richardson Resort &**

Marina (Emerald Bay Road; 530-541-1777) and **Meeks Bay Marina** (7901 West Lake Boulevard, Tahoma; 530-525-7242). If you have your own boat, you'll find launch ramps north of Tahoma at **Homewood Marina** (5190 West Lake Boulevard, Homewood; 530-525-5966) and **Obexer's Boat Company** (5355 West Lake Boulevard, Homewood; 530-525-7962.

SKIING

Larger than it looks from below, **Homewood Mountain Resort** used to be two separate ski areas, and its 56 runs sprawl across 1260 acres of terrain with a maximum vertical drop of 1650 feet. Although it has little snowmaking capacity, its West Shore location has some of the best fresh powder in the region soon after snowstorms. About 85 percent of the runs are rated intermediate or advanced, including a challenging back bowl. Not only is snowboarding allowed, there are special 'boarding classes for mature adults and seniors at the resort's terrain park above the quad lift. Standard and high-performance ski rental packages are available, as well as snowboard rentals. ~ 5145 West Lake Boulevard, Homewood; 530-525-2992, snow conditions 530-525-2900; www.skihomewood.com, e-mail smile@skihomewood.com.

Camp Richardson is the headquarters for most Nordic skiing on the West Shore. The **Camp Richardson Cross-country Ski Center** maintains 35 kilometers of trails along the lake and offers ski rentals and lessons. Skiers can also tour the 3-kilometer loop trail around nearby Tallac Historic Site and national forest trails

SKIING INTO YESTERYEAR

To experience skiing the way it used to be, try out **Granlibakken**, Lake Tahoe's oldest ski area. This tiny ski run—just 280 feet vertical drop with two runs, mostly for beginners, and a single poma lift—dates back to 1927. It was built in 1927 and served for decades as a training area for Olympic ski jumpers. The old ski jump still looms over the slopes, though it is no longer in use. Lift tickets are by far the least expensive in the Lake Tahoe region. Snowboarding is allowed, and there is a snow play area for sleds and saucers. Snowboards and saucer sleds are available for rent. ~ 725 Granlibakken Road; 530-581-7533, 800-543-3221; www.granlibakken.com.

such as the **Fallen Leaf Dam Trail** (4-kilometer loop). ~ Camp Richardson Resort, Emerald Bay Road; 530-541-1801, 800-544-1801, fax 530-541-1802; www.camprichardson.com.

CAMPING

Motorhome travelers swear by **Historic Camp Richardson Resort**, where for a surprisingly reasonable fee you can get one of the few full-hookup sites on the West Shore plus all the privileges of staying at a full-service resort. It's also the largest campground around, so tenters may want to consider all their options before pitching camp here. The 112 RV and 223 tent sites are semi-secluded in the woods a short distance from the lake. Campground amenities include picnic tables and restrooms with showers; a marina, boat launch facility, dump station, camp store, six-mile bike path, restaurant and nightclub, as well as Tallac Historic Site and the Taylor Creek Visitors Center, are just a short stroll away. No pets. Sites cost $23 to $29 per night. Open May to mid-October. ~ Emerald Bay Road; 530-541-1801, 800-544-1801, fax 530-541-1802; www.camprichardson.com.

In the same area, across the road from Tallac Historic Site, the National Forest Service's **Fallen Leaf Campground** sits on the wooded shore at the north end of the long, deep fishing lake of the same name. The 130 tent/RV sites have picnic tables, drinking water, a laundry room and outhouses but no hookups. Boat launch facilities are available. Sites cost $20 per night. Open May to mid-October. ~ Emerald Bay Road; 530-573-2674, reservations 877-444-6777, fax 630-573-2693.

Across the road from Emerald Bay, the National Forest Service's **Bayview Campground** is set in the woods just out of sight but not out of earshot of traffic. The trailhead for the scenic hike past Cascade Lake to White Cloud Falls makes this campground special, and its ten tent and small RV (under 20 feet) sites offer the only first-come, first-served camping on the lake. There are picnic tables, drinking water and outhouses but no hookups. Sites cost $10 per night, with a seven-night maximum stay. Open mid-May through September. ~ Emerald Bay Road; 530-544-5994.

The large but comfortably dispersed campground at **D.L. Bliss State Park** is set back in the forest near Rubicon Point at the north end of the park. It's more than half a mile away from the main road, and a lovely four-mile hiking loop starts at the campground and runs along the lake and back through the woods. There are 168 tent/RV sites (no motorhomes over 21 feet) with picnic tables, drinking water and restrooms with showers, but no hookups. Sites cost $20 to $30 per night. Open Memorial Day through Labor Day. ~ 530-525-7277, reservations 800-444-7275; www.reserveamerica.com.

The forest service's **Meeks Bay Campground** has a pretty lakefront location close to the main road. For bikers, joggers and rollerbladers, the best thing about this campground is its proximity to the start of a paved path that goes all the way to Tahoe City and Squaw Valley. There are 40 tent and small (under 20 feet) RV sites with picnic tables, drinking water and outhouses but no hookups. Sites cost $17 per night. Open mid-May to mid-October. ~ 530-583-3357, reservations 877-444-6777; www.reserveusa.com.

Directly across the cove from the forest service campground at Meeks Bay, the **Meeks Bay Resort**'s 24 tent and 10 RV sites (no motorhomes over 60 feet) share restrooms with showers and a laundromat, and some have full hookups. Boating and fishing are the resort's primary activities, so boat launch facilities and mooring docks are available. In addition, you'll find a swimming area, a camping store, a snack bar and a gift shop at the resort. Sites cost $20 to $30 per night, reservations required. Open April through October. ~ 530-525-6946, 877-326-3357.

In Sugar Pine Point State Park, the **General Creek Campground** is set deep in the pines, on the west side of the road more than a mile from the lake. The end of the main camping loop fronts on General Creek, where a picturesque loop trail follows the creek with its lush riparian flora for miles. The large campground has 175 tent/RV (up to 32 feet long) sites with

Camp Sites with Shine

On the high, wooded ridge along the south side of Emerald Bay, the campground at **Emerald Bay State Park** has perhaps the most beautiful setting of any campground on the Lake Tahoe Shore, looking down from Eagle Point to Vikingsholm Castle, Fannette Island and the vibrant, deep green water of the bay. After the cruise boats have departed the harbor and the castle visitors have left, you and your fellow campers will have the area all to yourselves to walk around the perimeter of the bay; get up early and you can hike the lakeshore Rubicon Trail to watch dawn break over the lake. There are 100 tent/RV sites (no motorhomes over 21 feet) with picnic tables, drinking water and restrooms with showers, but no hookups. There's also a 20-site first-come, first-served boat-in campground at the end of Eagle Point. Sites cost $15 to $20 per night. Open Memorial Day through Labor Day. ~ Emerald Bay Road; 530-525-7232, reservations 800-444-7925; www.reserveamerica.com.

picnic tables and restrooms with showers, but no hookups. Sites cost $20 per night. Open year-round. ~ 530-525-7982, reservations 800-444-7275; www.reserveamerica.com.

Tiny **Kaspian Campground** is set right by the water near the mouth of Blackwood Canyon and enjoys one of the best lake views on the West Shore; a 20-mile paved biking and jogging path runs right through it. This forest service campground has just nine tent sites, and small (under 20 feet) RVs can use the parking area on a space-available basis, first-come, first-served. There are picnic tables, drinking water and outhouses, but no hookups. Sites cost $15 per night. Open late May through September. ~ West Lake Boulevard; 530-583-3642, reservations 877-444-6777; www.reserveusa.com.

About two miles up the road is another forest service campground, **William Kent Camp**, surrounded by lodgepoles just off the west side of the busy roadway to nearby Tahoe City. Recent construction in the area puts this campground within walking distance, if not earshot, of the Tahoe City "suburbs." There are 51 tent sites and 40 sites for RVs up to 40 feet long, all with picnic tables but no hookups. There are restrooms, drinking water and a dumping station. Sites cost $16 per night. Open mid-May to mid-October. ~ West Lake Boulevard; 530-583-3642, reservations 877-444-6777; www.reserveusa.com.

lodging

The big kahuna on Lake Tahoe's West Shore, **Historic Camp Richardson Resort** is technically within the city limits of South Lake Tahoe but feels like a world apart. There are rooms in the spacious lodge near the lake as well as private cabins. The lodge lobby is vintage High Sierras, with knotty-pine walls, a high beam ceiling and a big rock fireplace. The decor of the 28 lodge guest rooms features rustic handmade furniture, while the 40 cabins—some secluded in the forest, others set right on the brink of the lake—are suitelike, with separate sitting areas furnished with fold-out sofas and Mexican *equipal* chairs; they have kitchens and big windows with huge views. There are also con-

Historic Camp Richardson Resort.

Granlibakken Resort

ventional motel-style units in the camp's Beachside Inn and two large units, each of which sleeps up to six, at the Marina Duplex. Guests have the use of a gazebo hot tub as well as access to the resort's many recreational facilities such as bike, boat and horse rentals. ~ Emerald Bay Road; 530-541-1801, 800-544-1801, fax 530-541-1802; www.camprichardson.com, e-mail info@camprichardson.com. MODERATE TO DELUXE.

You'll find 11 old-timey cabins nestled in sugar pine forest at **Tahoma Meadows Bed and Breakfast**. Individually decorated in motifs ranging from wildflowers to deep forest hues, the 14 cabin units have queen- or king-size beds. Many have clawfoot tubs, and some have kitchens and fireplaces. ~ 6821 West Lake Boulevard, Tahoma; 530-525-1533, 800-355-1596; www. tahoemeadows.com. MODERATE TO ULTRA-DELUXE.

Set in a pine forest several miles south of Tahoe City, **Sunnyside Lodge** carries a hunting theme throughout, with taxidermic trophies around the big river-rock fireplace in the lobby and ducks and decoys decorating the 23 lakeside or lakeview cabins. Each cabin is individually and eclectically furnished with wicker, hardwood and antiques. Many have fireplaces and wet bars. No pets. ~ 1850 West Lake Boulevard; 530-583-7200, 800-822-2754, fax 530-583-7224; www.sunnysideresort.com. DELUXE.

Granlibakken Resort has steadily expanded from its old-time ski lodge to a full conference center with 159 guest accommodations including suites and condominium units. All units have phones and TVs; some have fireplaces. Besides its tiny ski slope and snow play area, the resort has tennis courts, a spa and sauna, an outdoor swimming pool and trails for mountain biking in summer and cross-country skiing in winter. ~ 625 Granlibakken Road, Tahoe City; 530-583-4242, 800-543-3221; www.granlibakken.com, e-mail granresv@sierra.net. MODERATE TO DELUXE.

dining

The **Beacon Bar & Grill** at Historic Camp Richardson Resort offers indoor and outdoor dining for lunch and dinner, as well as a champagne brunch on Saturday and Sunday. The menu focuses on seafood, with such meals like macadamia nut–crusted salmon and Cajun blackened catfish. For landlubbers, the menu includes a handful of gourmet pork and beef dishes such as New York strip steak in whiskey peppercorn sauce. ~ Emerald Bay Road; 530-541-1801, 800-544-1801; fax 530-541-1802; www.camprichardson.com, e-mail info@camprichardson.com. DELUXE.

A breakfast favorite, the **Firesign Café** in Sunnyside features an eclectic array of alternatives to the usual bacon-and-eggs fare. Try the Cape Cod eggs Benedict, the *huevos rancheros* or the artichoke omelette. Also open for lunch with a selection of deli-style sandwiches. ~ 1785 West Lake Boulevard, Sunnyside; 530-583-0871. MODERATE.

The **Sunnyside Lodge Restaurant** has great views of the water and neighboring marina from both the outside deck and the indoor dining room. Seafood is the specialty, ranging from grilled salmon and mahimahi to mixed fish, calamari and crab fettuccini. This establishment's long-established rep-

YODELAY-HEE-HOO

One of Lake Tahoe's oldest restaurants, the **Swiss Lakewood Restaurant** has been operating continuously since 1919. The decor is as Swiss as Heidi's grandfather, and so are many of the menu choices such as Zurich-style veal and wienerschnitzel. There are also highly original entrées that blend Continental tradition with California nouveau flair, like escallops of venison with glazed chestnuts and balsamic vinegar lingonberry sauce. Dinner only. Closed Monday; closed weekdays in winter. ~ 5055 West Lake Boulevard, Homewood; 530-525-5211. ULTRA-DELUXE.

Beacon Bar & Grill at Historic Camp Richardson Resort.

utation surpasses its present-day cuisine, so reservations are essential. ~ 1850 West Lake Boulevard; 530-583-7200, 800-822-2754, fax 530-583-7224; www.sunnysideresort.com. DELUXE.

nightlife

After the dinner hour, there's live jazz or blues in the **Beacon Bar & Grill** at Historic Camp Richardson Resort—just about the only evening entertainment option on this side of the lake. ~ Emerald Bay Road; 530-541-1801, 800-544-1801; www.camprichardson.com. DELUXE.

The **Taylor Creek Visitors Center** has an outdoor amphitheater where special programs are presented on Monday, Wednesday, Thursday and Friday evenings during the summer. Programs feature slide shows, stories and legends about Lake Tahoe's history, and some present live one-man stage impersonations of historical figures such as John Muir and Mark Twain. ~ Lake Tahoe Basin Management Unit, 530-573-2674; www.r5.fs.fed.us/ltbmu.

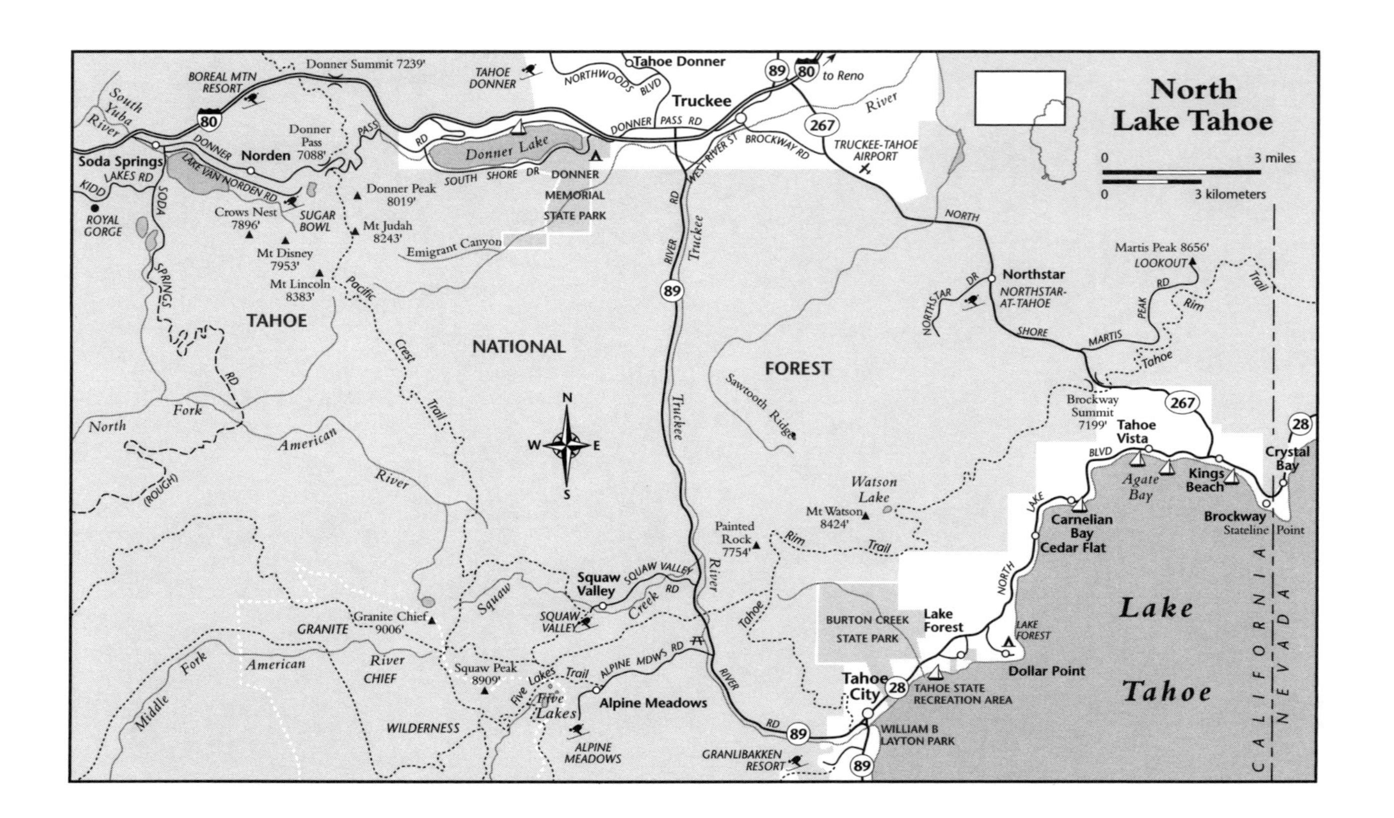
North Lake Tahoe
0 3 miles
0 3 kilometers
Tahoe Donner
Truckee
to Reno
Donner Summit 7239'
BOREAL MTN RESORT
TAHOE DONNER
South Yuba River
Soda Springs
Norden
Donner Pass 7088'
Donner Lake
DONNER MEMORIAL STATE PARK
Donner Peak 8019'
Mt Judah 8243'
Crows Nest 7896'
SUGAR BOWL
Mt Disney 7953'
Mt Lincoln 8383'
ROYAL GORGE
Emigrant Canyon
TRUCKEE-TAHOE AIRPORT
TAHOE
NATIONAL
FOREST
Pacific Crest Trail
North Fork American River
Sawtooth Ridge
Northstar
NORTHSTAR-AT-TAHOE
Martis Peak 8656'
LOOKOUT
Tahoe Rim Trail
Brockway Summit 7199'
Tahoe Vista
Agate Bay
Kings Beach
Crystal Bay
Brockway
Stateline Point
Carnelian Bay
Cedar Flat
Watson Lake
Mt Watson 8424'
Painted Rock 7754'
Truckee River
Squaw Valley
SQUAW VALLEY
Squaw Creek
Granite Chief 9006'
GRANITE CHIEF WILDERNESS
Squaw Peak 8909'
Five Lakes
Alpine Meadows
ALPINE MEADOWS
Middle Fork American River
BURTON CREEK STATE PARK
Lake Forest
LAKE FOREST
Dollar Point
Tahoe City
TAHOE STATE RECREATION AREA
WILLIAM B LAYTON PARK
GRANLIBAKKEN RESORT
Lake Tahoe
CALIFORNIA
NEVADA
NORTHWOODS BLVD
DONNER PASS RD
WEST RIVER ST
BROCKWAY RD
LAKE VAN NORDEN RD
KIDD LAKES RD
SODA SPRINGS RD
SOUTH SHORE DR
RIVER RD
NORTH SHORE
NORTHSTAR DR
MARTIS PEAK RD
NORTH LAKE BLVD
SQUAW VALLEY RD
ALPINE MDWS RD
(ROUGH)
80
89
267
28

8

North Lake Tahoe

A stroll down North Lake Boulevard, Tahoe City's main street, reveals the split personality of the North Shore area. On one side of the street, sailboat masts sway gently at the marina docks and beachgoers bask on the sandy strands along the lake shore. Only a chain-link fence separates sunbathers from the motorists trapped in the traffic snarls that are typical on summer weekends. On the other side of the street, icicle Christmas lights drip year-round from the rooflines of some of the restaurants, lodges and shops built in the architectural style usually associated with international ski resorts. One could feel right at home dressed in bathing trunks, flip-flops and a ski parka.

Tahoe City, not really much of a "city" with its population of only 1100, has a long, spotty heritage. It got its start in the last decades of the 19th century, when the only way to reach the exclusive resort hotels and elegant summer homes along Lake Tahoe's South and West shores was to ride a train from San Francisco to the town of Truckee. From there, a narrow-gauge railroad chugged up the Truckee River for 14 miles to Tahoe City, where paddlewheel steamboats waited to carry passengers to their destinations across the lake. But as 20th-century automobile roads made it easier to reach the lake and the old haunts of the wealthy gave way to more "modern" resorts like Historic Camp Richardson, Tahoe City was largely eclipsed by South Lake Tahoe.

Then in 1955, Tahoe City's luck changed as nearby Squaw Valley, a fledgling local ski area with one rope tow and four double chairlifts, was chosen to be the site of the VIII Winter Olympics in 1960. Fortunes were invested in transforming Squaw Valley into an Olympic complex that could host, among other events, ski races, ski jumping, speed skating and hockey matches, with an Olympic Village that

Opposite: Ice rink at Squaw Valley.

could accommodate 1000 competitors and 20,000 spectators. The largest Winter Olympics ever held up to that time and the first to be televised nationally, it introduced Americans to the sport of alpine skiing and instantly established Squaw Valley's reputation as one of the world's great ski resorts, setting the standard by which other ski areas such as Aspen, Vail and—yes—Heavenly Lake Tahoe would be judged. Today Squaw Valley still ranks as a premier ski resort. Sky cranes seem to be permanent fixtures, attesting to the valley's continuous growth. The 12 ski slopes located within a half-hour's drive of Tahoe City comprise more than half of all alpine ski areas in California.

The other aspect of the North Shore miracle is that, through it all, Tahoe City and its neighboring communities have clung to their friendly, hometown feel. Don't expect to find big, impersonal, brand-name resort lodges along the North Shore; the largest motor inns have around 50 guest rooms, and most lodgings run between a dozen and 20 units.

sightseeing

As you enter Tahoe City from the south, you'll cross **Fanny Bridge** over the Truckee River, Lake Tahoe's only outlet. The bridge got its name because there are almost always people leaning over its concrete railing, posteriors skyward, to see the giant rainbow trout that have grown accustomed to being fed from the bridge. You can also see the Lake Tahoe outlet gates, which control the flow of water into the Truckee River to regulate the water levels in both the lake and the river.

On the south bank of the river next to the bridge is the municipal **William B. Layton Park**, a pine-shaded plot of land on which the main feature is the **Gatekeeper's Museum**. Built from lodgepole pines by the North Lake Tahoe Historical Society, the museum stands on the foundation of the Gatekeeper's Cabin, where the watermasters who controlled the floodgates from the lake into the river lived from 1913 to 1968. Although the outlet is still controlled by a federal employee who raises and lowers the gates by hand, the original cabin was destroyed by fire in 1978. The on-site museum contains vintage photographs, history displays and a research library, as well as models of old-time ski equipment and steamboats that used to carry passengers across the lake. One wing of the building houses the **Marion Steinback Indian Basket Museum**, a collection of more than 800 baskets representing 85 tribes along with other native artifacts such as dolls, pot-

Skating on Top of the World

Even when there's no snow on the slopes, you can find high adventure at Squaw Valley. In summer, activities focus on **High Camp**, a recreation complex at the top of a scenic cable car ride that climbs 2000 feet for a fabulous view of the valley and the rugged granite peaks beyond. The year-round outdoor ice-skating pavilion is located at the top of the cable car ascent, as are the swimming lagoon, spa and tennis courts. Tickets for any or all of these activities, including cable car transportation, cost only slightly more than the cable car ride alone. Also at the cable car summit, the Adventure Center and Climbing Wall has a 30-foot indoor simulated rock climbing wall and a 45-foot outdoor wall. ~ Squaw Valley; 530-583-6955, 800-545-5350, climbing wall 530-583-7673; www.squaw.com.

tery, gambling trays and caribou hoof rattles. The museum is open Wednesday through Sunday from May through September, daily from mid-June through Labor Day. ~ 130 West Lake Boulevard, Tahoe City; 530-583-1762.

Just up the street, the **North Tahoe Art Center** stands on land deeded to the citizens of Tahoe City by President Ulysses S. Grant. At various times, the historic building here has served as the town's post office, library and community center. Today it exhibits works by area artists who operate it as the nonprofit, volunteer-run Tahoe Artists' Network. Closed Tuesday. ~ 380 North Lake Boulevard, Tahoe City; 530-581-2787.

Right in the middle of Tahoe City's lakefront, **Tahoe City Commons Beach** is a large, grassy "beach"—some might call it a town park—with a children's playground and plenty of locals hanging out in summer. Above the beach stands the **Watson Cabin Living Museum**, the oldest building in Tahoe City, dating back to 1909. Daily except Tuesday in season, docents conduct tours of the cabin, which still has some of its original furniture. Lilacs surrounding it are said to have been planted by the original occupants. The beach and cabin are open from Memorial Day weekend through Labor Day weekend. No dogs. ~ 530-583-8717.

Half a mile east of the Tahoe City "wye" (the junction of Route 89 and Route 28 at Fanny Bridge, locally written as "wye" to avoid confusion with South Lake Tahoe's "Y"), **Tahoe State Recreation Area** is a 62-acre pocket park with an unattractive patch of lakefront and a shady picnic area with restrooms. Day-use fee. ~ Route 28, Tahoe City; 530-525-7232, fax 530-525-6730; www.agency.resource.ca.gov/parks/dpr.

Sooner or later, you'll want to take an orientation drive through the other small communities that dot the north shore on Route 28, but first, why not take a drive north along the **Truckee River**? You'll find that there's more to Tahoe than the lake itself. The river ripples its lazy way below the foot of Thunder Cliffs, with an inviting bike path—a continuation of the one that follows the West Shore up from Meeks Bay—along its bank.

You can't miss the turnoff on your left to **Squaw Valley**. The 79-foot-tall, 29-foot-wide **Tower of Nations** left over from the 1960 Winter Olympics marks the road with its giant Olympic rings and the crests of the 34 nations that participated in the Winter Games that year. In a box canyon ringed by towering mountains, the valley is a broad, pastoral jewel with a huge and growing recreation village at the upper end. ~ Squaw Valley; 530-583-6955, 800-545-5350; www.squaw.com.

Continuing north on Route 89 along the Truckee River, you'll soon come to **Truckee**, population 2400, at the junction

Skiers at Squaw Valley.

Bad Times in Truckee

In the annals of lawless old towns, few can compare with Truckee. Once four times its present size, the majority of its population was made up of Chinese workers and their families who had come to the area while building the railroad. White townspeople of the day resented them, and in 1876 a mob rampaged through the town, burning Chinese homes and shooting people. Virtually all of the Chinese residents left town after that incident, which came to be known as the Trout Creek Outrage. Truckee's vigilantes became the nucleus of a white supremacist group called the Order of Caucasians and had 10,000 members throughout the Gold Country by the time it was abolished 15 years later.

Downtown Truckee.

All that was in the past when Prohibition came along in the 1920s. Under the protection of local law enforcement, Truckee's saloons operated openly throughout Prohibition, and the town gained a reputation as the liquor and gambling capital of the Sierra; the bootlegging business here is said to have been the biggest on the West Coast. Wide-open defiance of the law attracted many Roaring Twenties desperados, and at one time or another Truckee's saloons and jail were visited by "Baby Face" Nelson, "Pretty Boy" Floyd, "Machine Gun" Kelly, Alvin Karpis and the Ma Spinelli Gang. Oddly enough, in the same era, Truckee also became a favorite location for Hollywood movie productions.

with busy Interstate 80. This 19th-century town is set atop a 5820-foot mountain pass, where its original residents provided water, firewood and ice to the steamtrains that succeeded in chugging their way up the steep grade that took them from Sacramento over the Sierra Nevada. Authentic Old West buildings, along with clapboard warehouses and meeting halls with second-story balconies, line Commercial Street, the town's main historic district, which is well-preserved though gentrified with art galleries and trendy restaurants.

Start your exploration of the town at the **Old Truckee Jail Museum**, run by the Truckee-Donner Historical Society. You'll find historic photos of Truckee's heyday as well as old-time ice-harvesting equipment and ski gear and relics from its Chinese heritage. You can also get a historic walking tour brochure there that will guide you around Truckee to see such historic buildings as Gray's Log Cabin (the oldest building in town), the Truckee Hotel, and the Rocking Stone Tower; the 17-ton stone, now cemented into place, used to rock with the touch of a finger. ~ 10142 Jibboom Street, Truckee; 530-582-0893.

Donner Memorial.

Two miles west of Truckee, **Donner Memorial State Park** is set in a pine and fir forest beside Donner Lake. Just about every schoolchild growing up in the American West learns the grisly tale of the Donner Party, a group of pioneers from the Midwest who took an unexplored "shortcut" that added weeks to their trip and ended up trapped by early snows in the High Sierra. Of the 89 people who started the journey, only 48 remained alive when rescue finally came, more than five months later. The survivors had lived by eating ox hides and, later, their dead friends and relatives. Today, the base of the Donner Memorial is 22 feet high—the same as the depth of the snow that accumulated during that terrible win-

A Party Remembered

Located in Donner Memorial State Park, the **Emigrant Trail Museum** details the Donner Party story with photographs of old journals as well as artifacts ranging from William Foster's rifle to Tamsen Donner's chinaware. Ironically, the pass where the Donner Party was trapped was eventually chosen as the best route for Interstate 80, which carries some 15,000 cars and trucks a day over the crest of the Sierra Nevada. (Tire chains may be required in winter.) Admission. ~ Donner Pass Road, Truckee; 530-582-7892, fax 530-582-7893.

ter. ~ Donner Pass Road, Truckee; 530-582-7892, fax 530-582-7893; www.ceres.ca.gov/sierradsp/donner.html.

Also at Donner Pass, in the Boreal ski area eight miles west of Truckee, the Auburn Ski Club's **Western America Ski Sport Museum** traces the history of skiing in the High Sierra, from the adventures of "Snowshoe" Thompson, who delivered the mail on skis from the 1850s through the 1870s, to the skiing boom brought about by the 1960 Winter Olympics at Squaw Valley. Old skiing movies are shown on weekends. Open Wednesday through Sunday. ~ Boreal Mountain Playground; 530-426-3313.

Returning from Truckee to Tahoe City, head east along North Lake Boulevard (Route 28). The road follows the shore for 11 miles to the Nevada state line, as wooded ridgelines separate small lakefront communities (**Lake Forest**, **Cedar Flat** and **Carnelian Bay**); the vintage vacation cabin compounds of **Tahoe Vista**; and the area's commercial center (which is to say, a gas station and a supermarket), **Kings Beach**. Though there are small sand beaches along the waterfront in Lake Forest and Tahoe

Vista, the main public beach along this drive is at **Kings Beach State Recreation Area**, where you'll also find picnic areas, restrooms, showers and a children's playground. No dogs. ~ 530-546-7248; www.northlaketahoe.net, e-mail ntpud@jps.net.

outdoor adventures

HIKING

Distances listed for all trails are one way unless otherwise noted. **Tahoe Rim Trail** is a 165-mile loop trail around the Tahoe Basin linking nine trailheads. The easiest to reach of all the access points are the two Tahoe City trailheads—the north trailhead located across from the community center on Fairway Drive just north of the "wye," and the south trailhead on the west side of Route 89, an eighth-mile south of the

Tracking the Chief

On first impression, it doesn't look as if you could climb out of the upper end of Squaw Valley, but in fact it is possible—and strenuous, with an elevation gain of 2700 feet in 3.5 miles. From the trailhead for the **Granite Chief Trail**, next to the Squaw Valley fire station, the trail switchbacks along ridgelines to the headwaters of the Middle Fork of the American River. You'll pass two sparkling mountain springs before starting up another set of switchbacks to a saddle from which you can scramble to the 8950-foot summit of Tinker Knob for a panoramic view of Squaw Valley and the Granite Chief Wilderness. From here, if you want a longer hike you can continue for 3.3 more miles to the wilderness boundary, where the Granite Chief Trail intersects the Pacific Crest Trail and provides access to more than 40 miles of trails to every corner of the wilderness area.

"wye." From the north trailhead, the rim trail goes through 18.5 miles of aspen and evergreen forest, alternating with open hillside meadows, along the south slope of Mount Watson and past Watson Lake to **Brockway Summit**, located along Route 267 north of Kings Beach. For a short hike, take the first two miles of the rim trail—a rocky switchback climb with an elevation gain of 880 feet—to a lookout point with a beautiful view of the lake.

One of the most popular hikes in the North Shore area, the 2.5-mile **Five Lakes Trail** starts at a marked trailhead along Alpine Meadows Road. From the Tahoe City "wye," take Route 89 north toward Truckee for 3.6 miles and turn left toward Alpine Meadows ski area; go 2.2 miles and you'll find the trailhead in a residential area near the intersection with Deer Park Drive. The first part of the trail climbs steeply up a series of switchbacks through the woods. Then you break out of the forest to find yourself among imposing granite rock formations with a view of the ski area below. Farther along, you come to the boundary of the Granite Chief Wilderness at the edge of a Douglas fir forest. Soon one of the Five Lakes (which have no individual names) comes into view. A spur trail takes you among the other four pretty little alpine lakes. No bikes.

High on Lake Tahoe

Visitors who like their vacation plans up in the air have a variety of options. **Lake Tahoe Parasailing** lifts you as high as 1400 feet above the surface of the lake, using tandem parachutes that can carry a couple or a parent and child. ~ 700 North Lake Boulevard, Tahoe City; 530-583-7245; www.laketahoeaquasports.com. **Mountain High Balloons** conducts half-hour and one-hour early-morning flights that take you high over Lake Tahoe and dip down so close to the treetops that you can pick pinecones. ~ Truckee; 530-587-6922. You can go bungee jumping at Squaw Valley's **High Camp**, located at the upper cable car station. ~ 530-583-4000. You can learn to fly through the air with the greatest of ease 25 feet above the ground with an instructor and professional catcher at **Gallagher's Flying Trapeze**. ~ 3225 North Lake Boulevard, Tahoe City; 530-308-6452. And **Skydive Lake Tahoe** not only offers complete instruction courses but lets first-time jumpers experience the thrill of a 60-second freefall in a tandem jump with a professional instructor. ~ Nervino Airport; 530-832-1474; www.skydivelaketahoe.com.

Near Truckee, the 4.5-mile **Mount Judah Loop Trail** starts at the parking area off Donner Pass Road (old Route 40), which leaves the interstate at Donner Lake. Take the Pacific Crest Trail south for one mile, climbing steeply up a granite headwall and then gradually moderating to a gentler climb. One mile south of the trailhead, turn left onto the Judah Loop Trail, which continues to climb to a four-wheel-drive road near Coldstream Pass between Mount Judah and Donner Peak. Turn left onto this primitive road, and almost immediately you'll find yourself in a wet alpine area that has fantastic displays of wildflowers in the spring and early summer. Shortly the trail resumes on the south side of the road and climbs the northeast face of Mount Judah, making its way to the summit of the 8243-foot mountain, which is part of the Sugar Bowl ski area. As you hike along the mountain's top ridge, you get views of the surrounding mountains, Donner Lake and Truckee. As it leaves the crest, the trail descends to a point just north of Roller Pass, a route used by '49ers to take their covered wagons over the Sierra. Signs tell the story of the fearsome challenges the pioneers encountered in trying to make their way up the forbidding cliff. Here, you rejoin the Pacific Crest Trail for the return trip to the parking area on Donner Pass.

TRUCKIN' DOWN THE TRUCKEE

Whether you rent a raft or choose to hang ten on a giant inner tube, the Truckee River north from Tahoe City is a generally quiet rafting ride punctuated by small rapids, riffles and pools. Float trips are available from May through September whenever the river level is high enough. Contact the **Truckee River Raft Company** (185 River Road, Tahoe City; 530-581-0123) or **Truckee River Rafting** (55 West Lake Boulevard, Tahoe City; 530-583-7238).

BIKING

A wide, essentially level paved bike path links to the West Shore Bike Path from Meeks Bay (see Chapter 7) and follows the Truckee River for 4.5 miles north to Squaw Valley. Another branch of the same path parallels North Lake Boulevard for 3 miles through Tahoe City to North Lake Tahoe High School in Lake Forest.

In summer, **Squaw Valley** is a great place for bikers of all skill levels, with a paved bike path that connects to the one along the Truckee River as well as a mountain bike park with a maze of unpaved roads and trails. In addition, you can take your mountain bike on the cable car to High Camp for easy access to trails above 8000 feet in elevation, as well as a 2000-foot descent on one of the resort's ski trails. Helmets are required, as is a trail pass, sold at all valley sporting equipment shops. Mountain bike and rollerblade rentals are available at the **Squaw Valley Sport Shop** (201 Squaw Valley Road; 530-583-3356), the **Granite Chief SkiService Center** (1602 Squaw Valley Road; 530-583-2832) and the **Resort at Squaw Creek** (400 Squaw Creek Road; 530-581-6694).

Biking along the Truckee River.

Mountain biking is allowed on the Tahoe Rim Trail in both directions from **Brockway Summit Trailhead** on Route 267 between Kings Beach and Truckee. If you go east from the summit, you can climb five miles to the old fire lookout near the top of 8742-foot **Martis Peak** via the rim trail, with a 1540-foot elevation gain, and then coast back down on paved Martis Peak Road. You can't go much beyond Martis Peak, though, before you come to the boundary of the Mount Rose Wilderness, where bikes are prohibited.

If you take the Tahoe Rim Trail west from Brockway Summit, you can ride 18.5 miles to the "wye" in Tahoe City. This ride starts at 7200 feet elevation, climbs gradually to a maximum of 7750 feet and then drops to 6200 feet at the Lake Tahoe shore. It travels through evergreen forest nearly all the way, breaking out sometimes into open glades and bare, sunny south-facing slopes. Landmarks along the trail are Watson Lake, Mount Watson and Painted Rock. For much of the way, it parallels partly paved Route 73, a former forest road that gives access to almost a dozen unpaved roads that also offer good biking possibilities.

Bicycle rentals are available on the North Shore at **The Back Country** (255 North Lake Boulevard, Tahoe City; 530-581-5861), **Olympic Bike Shop** (620 North Lake Boulevard, Tahoe City; 530-581-2500), **Enviro-Rents** (6873 North Lake Boulevard, Tahoe Vista; 530-546-2780) and **Tahoe Bike & Ski** (8499 North Lake Boulevard, Kings Beach; 530-546-7437)

BOATING AND RAFTING

Kayaking is popular on the North Shore, particularly in Agate Bay, off Tahoe Vista and Kings Beach. From there you can paddle east to **Brockway Point**, where giant boulders create a labyrinth of waterways, and around the point to Crystal Bay. Local water sports businesses have literally hundreds of kayaks for rent, and on a warm summer weekend you may see all of them out on the water at the same time. Rent your kayak at **Tahoe City Kayak** (1355 North Lake Boulevard, Tahoe City), the **Kayak Café & Rentals** (5166

North Lake Boulevard, Carnelian Bay; 530-546-9337), **Enviro-Rents** (6873 North Lake Boulevard, Tahoe Vista; 530-546-2780) or **Tahoe Paddle & Oar** (8299 North Lake Boulevard, Kings Beach; 530-581-3029).

If your taste runs to something noisier, you can rent a powerboat at **Tahoe City Marina** (700 North Lake Boulevard, Tahoe City; 530-583-1039) or **North Tahoe Marina** (7360 North Lake Boulevard, Tahoe Vista; 530-546-8248. These and other marinas along the North Shore also provide boat launch facilities.

One-, two- and three-person jet skis and Sea-Doos are available for rent at **Tahoe Water Adventures** (120 Grove Street, Tahoe City; 530-583-3225) and **Tahoe Aquatic Center** (8290 North Lake Boulevard, Kings Beach; 530-546-2419).

Private and semi-private sailing lessons are offered by the **Tahoe Sailing Academy** (5166 North Lake Boulevard, Carnelian Bay; 530-412-2628).

FISHING

You can arrange a sportfishing charter to take you out on Lake Tahoe in search of giant Mackinaw trout by contacting **Reel Deal Sportfishing** (Tahoe City; 530-581-0924), **Mickey's Big Mack Charters** (Carnelian Bay; 530-546-4444) or **Mac-A-Tac Fishing Charters** (Tahoe Vista; 530-546-2500). **Reel Magic Sportfishing** (Tahoe City; 530-587-6027) even offers a quasi-guarantee: no fish, no pay. Of course, they're not guaranteed to be *big* fish.

Anglers favor the Truckee River from 1000 feet below Lake Tahoe (you're not allowed to fish any closer to the lakeshore than that) down to Alpine Meadows Road. Stocked with rainbow trout, the river also has natural populations of brown trout and mountain whitefish. The only trouble is, the best fishing season—July and August—coincides with the peak river-rafting season, so flyfishing there can sometimes feel a little like playing golf in the middle of a freeway. The best strategy is to get out early in the morning or near sunset, when the river traffic subsides. For tackle and advice, drop in at **Mother Nature's**. ~ 551 North Lake Boulevard, Tahoe City; 530-581-4278.

West of Truckee, **Donner Lake** is very popular among anglers, with both shore fishing for abundant rainbow trout and kokanee salmon and deep-water fishing for Mackinaw trout. Be warned, however, that the lake is also popular among water skiers and jet skiers, who create a turmoil that (if you adopt the proper attitude) adds to the sporting challenge or (if you don't) feels a lot like having hornets nest in your head. Contact **Truckee River Outfitters & Fly Shop**. ~ 10200 Donner Pass Road, Truckee; 530-582-0900.

GOLF

Hidden away behind the Albertson's supermarket at the "wye" in Tahoe City, next to Fanny Bridge and across the street from the lakeshore, **Tahoe City Golf Course** is the oldest golf course at Lake Tahoe, built in 1917. Though short, the 2696-yard, nine-hole, 33-par course was a favorite

of such visiting celebrities as Bob Hope, Bing Crosby and Frank Sinatra in the days before Lake Tahoe had championship courses. Cart and club rentals are available, and there are a driving range and putting and chipping greens. Open April through November. ~ 251 North Lake Boulevard, Tahoe City; 530-583-1516.

Golf course designer Robert Trent Jones, Jr., revealed a sadistic streak when he laid out the golf course for the **Resort at Squaw Creek**. The back nine of this 18-hole, 6921-yard, par-71 course is essentially one big water hazard, a wetland so swampy that golfers have to drive their carts on wooden boardwalks. To make matters worse, the greens are small, and if you miss one, your ball may vanish for good with a sickening "splotch" sound. Club rentals are available, and cart rentals are mandatory. Open June through October. ~ 400 Squaw Creed Road, Olympic Valley; 530-583-6300; www.squawcreek.com.

A COURSE WITH HEART AND SOUL

A vintage nine-holer, the **Old Brockway Golf Course** is 3400 yards long and par 36. Built in 1924 as part of an elegant resort hotel that later burned down, the course hosted the first Bing Crosby Open golf tournament, and nicknames still in use for the various holes were said to have originated with the Rat Pack—Frank Sinatra, Dean Martin, Joey Bishop, Sammy Davis, Jr., and Peter Lawford—who were regular players here. Old Brockway is the only executive golf course in the western United States that has been designated an official wildlife sanctuary by the Audubon Society. Cart and club rentals are available. Open April through November. ~ 7900 North Lake Boulevard, Kings Beach; 530-546-9909; www.oldbrockway.com.

You have to wonder whether designer Robert Muir Graves was engaged in a nastiness contest with Jones when he built the **Northstar-at-Tahoe Golf Course**. This 18-hole, 6897-yard, par-72 course is downright manic-depressive. The front nine holes are a walk in the park, giving no hint that the back nine take you through a maze of water hazards, bunkers, narrow fairways between walls of dense pine forest and aspen groves, and tiny greens. Good luck. Cart and club rentals are available. Open May through October. ~ Midway between Truckee and Kings Beach on Route 267; 530-562-2490.

The only thing harder than playing the 18-hole, 6917-yard, par-72 **Tahoe Donner Golf Course** is getting a tee time there, because people who have homes in the surrounding residential development have priority and often make reservations far in advance. Hilly and filled with water hazards and solitary trees standing in the middle of fairways, the course is so full of tricks that the pro shop sells a special booklet on how to play it. There are a driving range and a putting green. Club rentals are available, and cart rentals are mandatory. Open mid-May to mid-September. ~ 12850 Northwoods Boulevard, Truckee; 530-587-9440; www.tahoedonner.com.

The longest golf course in the Truckee area, the 18-hole, 7177-yard, par-72 **Coyote Moon** presents challenges—distance drives, doglegs, three manmade lakes and a natural creek that meanders around seven holes—but no dirty tricks. Natural beauty is a key feature here, with big granite boulders and outcroppings and towering stands of Jeffrey pines. Club and cart rentals are available; use of carts is mandatory. Open May through October. ~ 10685 Northwoods Boulevard, Truckee; 530-587-0886.

HORSEBACK RIDING

During the summer months, several ski areas in the Tahoe City—Truckee area operate riding stables. **Alpine Meadows Stable** offers one-hour, two-hour and half-day rides through the surrounding forest and meadows, filled with wildflowers in spring. Deer and black bears are often spotted. Reservations are required for longer rides. ~ Alpine Meadows, Tahoe City; 530-583-3905.

Squaw Valley Stables takes groups on one- to three-hour rides around the perimeter of the valley. No reservations. ~ Squaw Valley; 530-583-7433. **Tahoe Donner Equestrian Center** offers guided trips that range from one hour to all day on 60 miles of trails through the surrounding pine forest; there are also night rides followed by a barbecue dinner every Saturday and on full-moon nights. Longer pack trips into the Castle Peak Wilderness can be arranged. Reservations are recommended. ~ Alder Creek Drive, Tahoe Donner; 530-587-

9470. **Northstar Stables** offers trail rides on the resort property year-round. Reservations are recommended. ~ Northstar-at-Tahoe, midway between Truckee and Kings Beach on Route 267; 530-562-1230.

SKIING

Lake Tahoe offers a wide choice of ski areas, each one distinctive and most relatively close together. If you're planning an all-week ski vacation, for maximum variety you may want to consider an interchangeable Ski Lake Tahoe lift ticket, good at Squaw Valley, Alpine Meadows, Northstar-at-Tahoe, Sierra-at-Tahoe, Kirkwood and Heavenly Lake Tahoe, available at all participating ski resorts.

Tahoe Area Regional Transit (TART) operates bus service to most ski areas around Tahoe City and Truckee from 6:30 a.m. to 6:30 p.m. daily. ~ 530-581-6365, 800-736-6365.

The closest large ski area to Tahoe City, **Alpine Meadows** covers both sides of Ward Peak and part of Scott Peak with 2100 skiable acres, more than 100 runs rated 25 percent beginner, 40 percent intermediate and 35 percent advanced. In addition, it has four big, untracked, off-the-beaten-path "adventure zones" rated most difficult to expert, two snowboard parks, a family "eco-trail," and a race course. Eleven chairlifts range from doubles to a six-passenger lift. The maximum vertical drop is 1800 feet. Unlike most other ski resorts in the North Shore/Truckee area, Alpine Meadows has views of Lake Tahoe from many runs. Standard and high-performance ski packages, snowboards, telemark skis and specialty equipment including snowshoes, short carvers and snowblades are available for rent. The resort offers lift-and-lodging packages with several participating local lodgings for just slightly more than the cost of lift tickets alone. Alpine Meadows also has one of the largest "adaptive" schools in North America for disabled skiers. ~ 2600 Alpine Meadows Road, Tahoe City; 530-583-4232, 800-441-4423; snow conditions 530-581-8374; skialpine.com, e-mail info@skialpine.com.

One of the world's great ski areas, **Squaw Valley** sprawls over six peaks with 4000 skiable acres, mostly wide-open bowls, and a vertical drop of 2850 feet. Runs are rated 25 percent beginner, 45 percent intermediate and 30 percent expert, plus there are two snowboard parks, a half pipe and a superpipe. There's also a special snow tubing area. Thirty chairlifts, including seven express lifts, take skiers up the mountains, and there are also a pulse lift, a 15-passenger cable car and North America's only Funitel gondola. The snow base averages 450 inches. Although adult tickets here are the most expensive on the North Shore, kids age 12 and under can ski for just $5. A number of ski rental packages, as well as snowboard rentals, are available. ~ Olympic Valley; 530-583-6955, 800-545-4350, snow conditions 888-766-9321; www.squaw.com, e-mail squaw@squaw.com.

Budget Bunny Slopes

Visitors with children in tow and/or looking for more bang for their buck have several choices aside from the big resorts. A small, family-oriented ski area with 41 runs on just 380 skiable acres, nine chairlifts and a vertical drop of 500 feet, **Boreal Mountain Resort** produces more manmade snow than any other ski resort in the region and thus is the first ski area to open each winter. The runs are rated 30 percent beginner, 55 percent intermediate and 15 percent expert. Low lift ticket prices and the wildly challenging Jibassic Terrain Park, plus two half-pipes, an easy family terrain zone and a nighttime-only terrain park, make Boreal a favorite place for snowboarders. Standard and high-performance ski packages and snowboards rentals are available. ~ Ten miles west of Truckee at Donner Summit; 530-426-3666; www.borealski.com.

Another small, low-cost ski slope, designed mainly for beginners' lessons, **Tahoe Donner** has just 125 acres of skiing in a single treeless bowl with a vertical drop of 600 feet. There are two chairlifts and a rope tow. Standard ski package rentals are available, and snowboarding is allowed. This is also a good place to try out a snow-bike, a pedal-powered vehicle with skis. Lessons for kids up to age 12 are free on weekdays. ~ 11509 Northwoods Boulevard, Truckee; 530-587-9444; www.tahoedonner.com, e-mail ski@tahoedonner.com.

Dating back to 1939, **Sugar Bowl** is the oldest large ski resort in the Lake Tahoe area and the site of the first chairlift in California. Today it spans 1500 skiable acres on four peaks—Mount Judah, Mount Lincoln, Mount Disney and Crow's Nest Peak—and has a 1500-foot vertical drop. The average snow base is a staggering 504 inches, one of the deepest accumulations in the Sierra Nevada. Nine chairlifts run from the central ski village and the Mount Judah parking area, and a gondola carries skiers from the main parking area to the village. The runs are 17 percent beginners, 43 percent intermediate and 40 percent expert. Among them is the Palisades, the steepest ski run in America. There are two terrain runs and a half-pipe for snowboarders, and ski and snowboard rentals are available. ~ Six miles west of Truckee on Route 267; 530-426-9000, snow conditions 530-426-1111; www.sugarbowl.com, e-mail info@sugarbowl.com.

Second in size only to Squaw Valley in the North Tahoe area, **Northstar-at-Tahoe** features 2420 skiable acres with 63

Royal Gorge.

runs, rated 25 percent beginner, 50 percent intermediate and 25 percent advanced, and an exceptional diversity of terrain. The vertical drop is 2280 feet from the summit of Mount Pluto to the ski village below; frequent skiers can get a unique Vertical Plus electronic lift ticket that calculates the total number of vertical feet you ski during the day and the season and gives you priority in lift lines. Snowboarding is allowed on all runs. Go during the week if possible—the lines at the gondola, eight chairlifts, two surface lifts and two Magic Carpets can be extremely long on weekends. ~ Midway between Truckee and Kings Beach on Route 267; 530-562-1010, snow conditions 530-562-1330; www.northstar.com, e-mail northstar@boothcreek.com.

Cross-country skiers will find an embarrassment of riches in the groomed trails around Tahoe City and Truckee. **Tahoe Cross Country Ski Area**, operated by the nonprofit Tahoe Cross Country Ski Education Association, maintains 65 kilometers of groomed trails through aspen and pine forest and across mountain meadows around the base of Mount Watson. Ski and snowshoe rentals are available. ~ Country Club Drive,

Tahoe City; 530-583-5475; www.tahoexc.org, e-mail info@tahoexc.org.

At Squaw Valley, the **Squaw Creek Cross Country Ski Center** has 30 kilometers of easy cross-country ski trails across the golf course fairways and open meadows on the valley floor. Ski and snowshoe rentals are available. ~ 400 Squaw Creek Road, Olympic Valley; 530-583-6300; www.squawcreek.com.

Northstar-at-Tahoe Cross Country and Telemark Ski Center starts at a lodge halfway up the mountain, reached by gondola, which serves as the hub for a 65-kilometer network of groomed trails for all skill levels, from the easy Sawmill Flat trail with a warming hut made from an old train caboose to an expert trail called the Black Hole. Cross-country and telemark ski rentals are available. ~ Midway between Truckee and Kings Beach on Route 267; 530-562-12475; www.northstar.com, e-mail northstar@boothcreek.com.

With 100 kilometers of groomed trails spanning 5000 acres, **Tahoe Donner Cross Country** is much larger than the nearby downhill ski area operated by the same folks. Trails range from easy loops like Pony Express to an ambitious climb up 7800-foot Donner Ridge, a favorite telemarking area. Cross-country, telemark ski and snowshoe rentals are available. Take a warmup break at the little snack bar colorfully named the Donner Party Café. ~ 11509 Northwoods Boulevard, Truckee; 530-587-9484; www.tahoedonner.com.

The largest cross-country ski area in America, **Royal Gorge—USA Cross Country Ski Resort** boasts 90 separate groomed trails totaling 330 kilometers in length—far more than most people could ski in a week. They range from gently undulating beginners' tracks to the harrowing Razorback Trail, which runs along the top of a narrow ridge with sheer dropoffs on both sides. One trail goes to nearby Sugar Bowl Ski Resort. An assortment of standard and high performance cross-country skis, telemark skis and snowshoes are for rent. ~ 9411 Hillside Drive, Soda Springs; 530-426-3871; www.royalgorge.com, e-mail info@royalgorge.com.

CAMPING

You get the advantage of being located close to everything—the lakefront, the shops and restaurants of Tahoe City and a paved bike route that will take you into town—when you camp at **Tahoe State Recreation Area**. The campsites are surrounded by a tall, thin stand of pine forest. There are 38 tent/RV sites with picnic tables, bear boxes and barbecues, but no hookups. There are restrooms, showers and drinking water. Sites cost $20 per night. Open May through October. ~ North Lake Boulevard, Tahoe City; 530-583-3074, reservations 800-444-7275; www.reserveamerica.com.

Lake Forest Campground was designed with boaters in mind, with a boat ramp and a wooded lakefront location near the point at the west end of Carnelian Bay. The point is also a good spot for trout fishing from shore. There are 20 tent/RV sites with picnic tables and barbecues plus drinking water and restrooms, but no hookups. Sites cost $15 per night, first-come, first-served. Open April through October. ~ Lake Forest Road, Lake Forest; 530-583-3796 ext. 29.

On scenic Brockway Point with its giant, half-sunken boulders offshore, the privately run **Sandy Beach Campground** is just a short walk from the casinos across the state line in Crystal Bay, Nevada. The 44 tent/RV sites can accommodate motorhomes up to 40 feet long, and 22 of them have full hookups. All sites have picnic tables and barbecues, and campground facilities include restrooms, showers and a laundry room. Sites cost $20 to $25 per night, reservations accepted.

Open May through October. ~ North Lake Boulevard, Brockway; 530-546-7682.

lodging

In dramatic contrast with the South Shore, the North Shore takes care of its tourist business on a mom-and-pop level and is proud of it.

A 1930s-era residence one block from the lake and an easy walk from the restaurants and shops of Tahoe City's main street, the **Mayfield House** bed and breakfast offers just six guest rooms, all with private baths. After a day of adventuring, you can relax with fellow guests in the comfortably furnished living room with its river-rock fireplace. ~ 236 Grove Street, Tahoe City; 530-583-1001, 888-518-8898, fax 530-581-4104; www.mayfieldhouse.com, e-mail innkeeper@mayfieldhouse.com. DELUXE TO ULTRA-DELUXE.

Blast from the Past

Back in the Roaring Twenties, when automobile roads first reached Lake Tahoe's North Shore, a new kind of lodging sprung up around the lake in competition with the exclusive luxury resorts of the South Shore. North Shore accommodations tended to be small clusters of cozy, self-contained vacation cabins secluded in the pines, most of them built from lumber cut locally and milled by the Brockway Lumber Company. In 1925, the lumber company itself was converted to vacation cottages, which were advertised as "Attractive and Clean—An Ideal Spot for Your Vacation—Center of All Activities—No Rattle Snakes, Poison Oak or Poison Ivy."

Later the Rustic Cottage Court deteriorated along with other North Shore cabin complexes—until the mid-1990s, when Janet and Marshall Tuttle bought them, set about renovating them into the kind of vacation lodgings they themselves sought when they traveled, and reopened them under the name **Rustic Cottage Resort & Motel**. Today the 18 cottages, which range from one-room cabins to spacious two-bedroom units with full kitchens and fireplaces, are completely renovated and furnished with Benicia iron beds handmade at the Tuttles' San Francisco furniture factory. Other modern conveniences include furnished outdoor decks, microwaves and televisions with HBO and VCRs to play selections from the extensive video library in the main office; however, there are no phones in the cabins. Set among towering pines just across the road from a sandy beach, it's one of the most relaxing places to stay in the whole Lake Tahoe area. ~ 7449 North Lake Boulevard, Tahoe Vista; 530-546-3523, 888-778-7892, fax 530-546-0146; www.rusticcottages.com, e-mail rustic@rusticcottages.com. MODERATE TO DELUXE.

You'll find six suites, each so spacious you could go hiking without ever stepping outside, at the **Tahoe Vista Inn & Marina**. Most have views of the lake, and all have separate bedrooms, kitchens and living rooms with stone fireplaces. A few have jacuzzis, too. The decor is tastefully muted soft gray and off-white, letting you feel colorful no matter what you wear. ~ 6647 North Lake Boulevard, Tahoe Vista; 530-546-2448. MODERATE TO ULTRA-DELUXE.

In contrast to the homey little lodgings found along Lake Tahoe's North Shore, in Squaw Valley the accommodations are stacked up until they look almost as high as the mountains themselves. A major ongoing lodge and condominium construction project is expanding the number of units for rent even as you read this, but for now the biggest facility, the **Resort at Squaw Creek**, offers 405 units: 387 one-bedroom suites and 18 two-bedroom suites, all with contemporary furnishings and kitchen facilities. The resort has two outdoor pools, as well as saunas, whirlpools, a skating rink and tennis courts, plus bicycle rentals, restaurants and retail shops. ~ 400 Squaw Creek Road, Olympic Valley; 530-583-6300, 800-404-9917, fax 530-581-5407; www.squawcreek.com. ULTRA-DELUXE.

Looking for something slightly smaller? The **Squaw Valley Lodge**, located at the foot of the ski slopes just 150 feet from the cable car, has 125 one- and two-bedroom suites with kitchens. The architecture and decor are European-style and alpine-inspired. There's a heated outdoor pool, as well as indoor

Tucked Inn History

If your idea of a great getaway includes a step back in time, look no farther than the **Truckee Hotel**. Painstakingly renovated, the four-story false-façade building dates back to 1868 and fills an entire block in the heart of the historic district. Like everything else in downtown Truckee, the hotel wears its checkered past on its sleeve. Rooms are furnished with antiques, and some are so authentic they even share bathrooms down the hall. ~ Corner of Bridge Street and Commercial Row, Truckee; 530-587-4444, 800-659-6921, fax 530-587-1599; www.thetruckeehotel.com, e-mail thetruckeehotel@sierra.net. MODERATE TO DELUXE.

Sun and Sand Lodge.

and outdoor whirlpool baths, a sauna and tennis courts. ~ 201 Squaw Peak Road, Olympic Valley; 530-583-5500, 800-765-3145, fax 530-583-0326; www.squawvalleylodge.com. ULTRA-DELUXE.

For lakefront lodgings in the North Shore's classic beach town, check out **Sun and Sand Lodge**, a 26-unit knotty-pine motel with one side of the property fronting on the sandy shore. The management is as friendly as can be. ~ 8308 North Lake Boulevard, Kings Beach; 530-546-2515, 800-547-2515, fax 530-546-0112. MODERATE TO DELUXE.

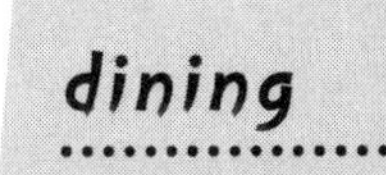

Italian food doesn't get any more authentic than the fare at **Bachi's Inn**, owned and operated by the same family for three generations. Red-and-white checkered tablecloths and dripping candles set the atmosphere for pastas and the house specialty, minestrone soup so tasty you may want to burst out with a verse or two of *O Solo Mio.* ~ 2905 Lake Forest Road, Tahoe City; 530-583-3324, fax 530-583-4924. MODERATE.

Owned by a Swiss family, **Tahoe House** is as European as can be in appearance, though its menu can best be described as California-Swiss fusion, ranging from fresh fish and home-

Le Petit Pier
RESTAURANT

FINE DINING

made pasta to veal dishes. The bakery, the real heart of this restaurant, sells fresh bread and pastries from early morning to late at night, and the desserts, redolent with real Swiss chocolate, are to die for. ~ Route 89, Tahoe City; 530-583-1377, 877-367-8246; www.tahoe-house.com, e-mail tahoehse@sierra.net. MODERATE TO DELUXE.

Billing itself as a "cuisine unique restaurant," **Wolfdale's** occupies a 1901 house on the lake shore. While the menu changes frequently, representative offerings include an appetizer of steamed artichoke with rock shrimp and entrées such as Thai tamarind seafood stew and filet mignon with wild mushroom ragôut. Dinner only. Closed Tuesday. ~ 640 North Lake Boulevard, Tahoe City; 530-583-5700, fax 530-583-1583; www.wolfdales.com. DELUXE.

Christy Hill got its start as the fanciest restaurant in Squaw Valley but later moved to its present chalet-style lakefront location in Tahoe City. Minimalist decor focuses diners' attention on the lake view through the wraparound windows in the dining room. The California cuisine features dishes like Anaheim *chiles rellenos* stuffed with smoked chicken and pepper jack cheese, broiled Australian lamb loin, and vegetarian choices such as baked eggplant parmesan topped with sautéed mushrooms, spinach and tomato pesto. Closed Monday. ~ 115 Grove Street, Tahoe City; 530-583-8551; www.christyhill.com, e-mail christyhill@tahoesbest.com. DELUXE.

Locals will tell you that the best breakfast on the beach is at the **Old Post Office Coffee Shop**, where country-style meat-and-eggs breakfasts, omelettes and pancakes start rolling off the griddle early in the morning and don't stop until the place closes after the noon hour. The lunch menu features chicken breast sandwiches and homemade chili *con carne.* ~ 5245 North Lake Boulevard, Carnelian Bay; 530-546-3205. BUDGET.

You don't have to speak a foreign language to order dinner at **Le Petit Pier**, but it helps. The menu selections range all the way from *filet sauté au poivre vert* to pheasant *souvaroff.* Black-tie waiters stand by to correct your pronunciation. Windows look out on the lake, white linen blankets the tables, and culinary award plaques cover the walls. Closed Tuesday and the first three weeks in November. ~ 7527 North Lake Boulevard, Tahoe Vista; 530-546-4464, fax 530-546-3272; www.lepetitpier.com. DELUXE TO ULTRA-DELUXE.

Fresh seafood highlights the bill of fare at **Captain Jon's**, a romantic dining establishment with dark wood appointments, white linen tablecloths, plenty of plants and a big stone fireplace. Entrées include salmon *en croûte*, scallops shiitake and lobster whiskey, accompanied by your selection from a long wine list. Closed three weeks in November. ~ 7220 North Lake Boulevard, Tahoe Vista; 530-546-4819, fax 530-546-7963. MODERATE TO DELUXE.

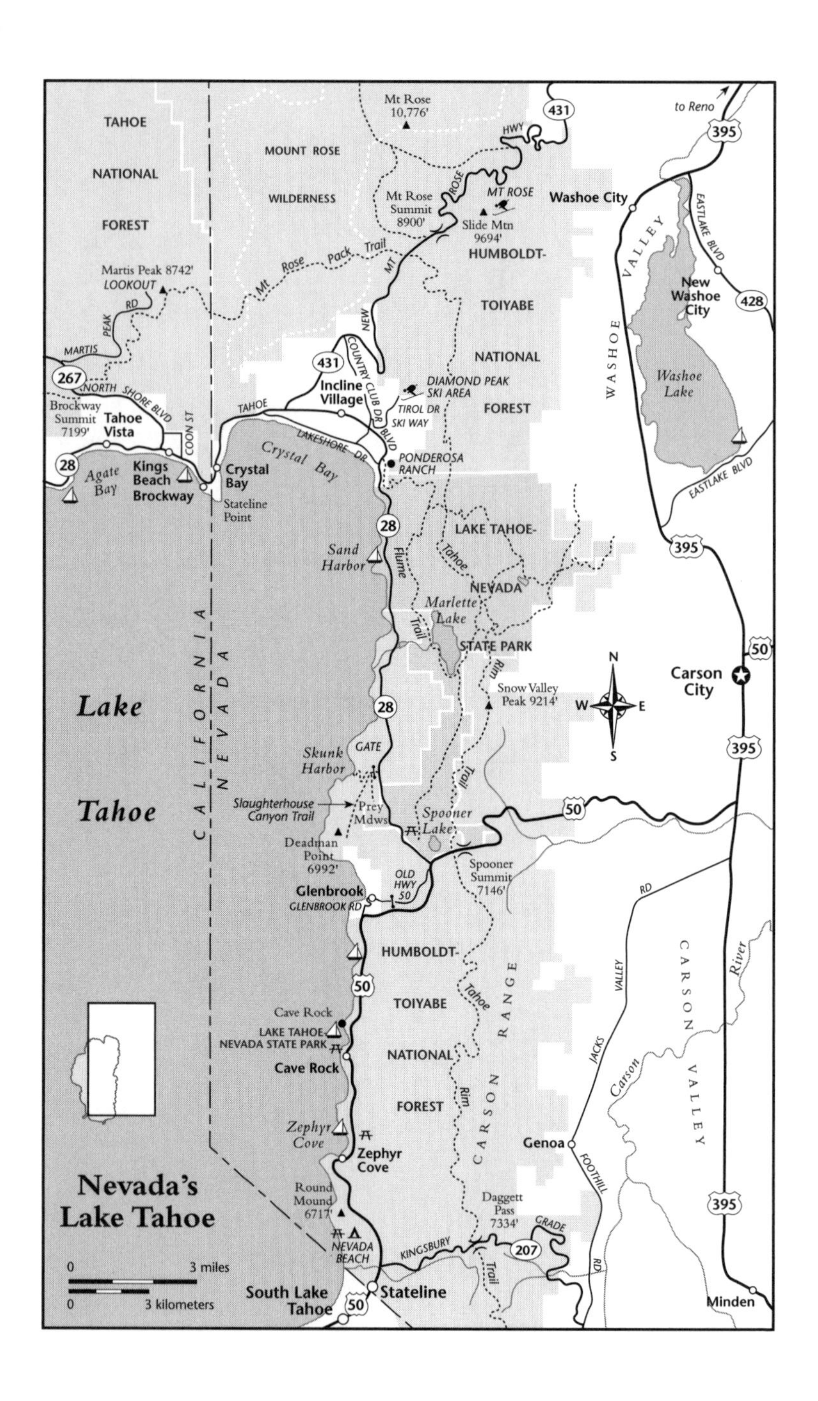
Nevada's Lake Tahoe
Lake Tahoe
TAHOE NATIONAL FOREST
MOUNT ROSE WILDERNESS
Mt Rose 10,776'
Mt Rose Summit 8900'
MT ROSE
Slide Mtn 9694'
HUMBOLDT-TOIYABE NATIONAL FOREST
Washoe City
to Reno
395
431
Mt Rose Pack Trail
Martis Peak 8742'
LOOKOUT
MARTIS PEAK RD
267
NORTH SHORE BLVD
Brockway Summit 7199'
Tahoe Vista
COON ST
28
Agate Bay
Kings Beach
Brockway
Crystal Bay
Stateline Point
Incline Village
COUNTRY CLUB DR
TAHOE BLVD
LAKESHORE DR
DIAMOND PEAK SKI AREA
TIROL DR
SKI WAY
PONDEROSA RANCH
New Washoe City
EASTLAKE BLVD
428
Washoe Lake
WASHOE VALLEY
LAKE TAHOE-NEVADA STATE PARK
Tahoe Rim Trail
Flume Trail
Sand Harbor
Marlette Lake
Snow Valley Peak 9214'
Carson City
50
CALIFORNIA
NEVADA
GATE
Skunk Harbor
Slaughterhouse Canyon Trail
Prey Mdws
Spooner Lake
Deadman Point 6992'
Spooner Summit 7146'
Glenbrook
GLENBROOK RD
OLD HWY 50
HUMBOLDT-TOIYABE NATIONAL FOREST
CARSON RANGE
Cave Rock
LAKE TAHOE-NEVADA STATE PARK
Zephyr Cove
JACKS VALLEY RD
Carson River
CARSON VALLEY
Genoa
FOOTHILL RD
Round Mound 6717'
Daggett Pass 7334'
KINGSBURY GRADE
207
NEVADA BEACH
South Lake Tahoe
Stateline
Minden
N
S
E
W
0
3 miles
3 kilometers

9

Nevada's Lake Tahoe

There are obvious differences between Lake Tahoe's East Shore and the rest of the lakefront. Being on the Nevada side of the state line, there are casinos. Instead of deep forests of lodgepole and Jeffrey pines, monoculture stands of ponderosas and bare grassy meadows bear witness to the extensive clearcutting that took place here during the area's silver mining boom in the late 19th century. Along much of the East Shore the slopes are so steep that the road winds hundreds of feet above the waterline, and there are even places where mountains plunge into the water so steeply that the shoreline can't be viewed or reached by land at all. Add to these the proximity of great skiing and hiking on Mount Rose, the sandy beaches of a large Nevada state park, golf courses, a popular recreational harbor and a legendary mountain bike trail, and you'll see why the Nevada side of the lake merits more attention than it usually receives from visitors.

sightseeing

Immediately upon crossing the California–Nevada state line on Route 28, motorists find themselves surrounded by a cluster of casino hotels. Although most of these places look as if they saw better days before Harrah's, Caesars and the big, glamorous casinos on the South Shore came along, they do boast interesting histories.

On the north side of the road, the **Tahoe Biltmore** is the oldest casino resort on the Nevada side of Lake Tahoe. The casino and the hotel were built by different owners in the 1940s; both were bought by a retired mobster formerly with Detroit's infamous Purple Gang. The hotel has been greatly enlarged, but the new additions are situated inconspicuously so that it retains its original appearance, a low stone and log lodge high on the hillside. ~ 5 Route 28, Crystal Bay; 775-831-0660, 800-245-8667; www.tahoebiltmore.com, e-mail fun@tahoebiltmore.com.

Just for Kids: Vintage Television Fun

Back in the early 1960s, "Bonanza" became the most popular TV Western show of all time and the first TV series ever to be broadcast regularly in color. It followed the adventures of widower Ben Cartwright and his three sons on their Nevada ranch, the Ponderosa, during the days of the Comstock Lode. After the series ended, the sets–both the Cartwrights' ranch and the town where much of the drama took place–were converted into **Ponderosa Ranch**, an Old West theme park in the hills above Incline Village. It seems strange that the kids who form the park's target market are far too young to remember the show; in fact, most of their parents are too young to remember it, too. But judging from the crowds that pack the park all summer, it's not really about the old TV series. Promoters have dreamed up a myriad ways to exploit the old shooting location (no pun intended). There are tours of the ranch house, video arcades and curio shops in the main street storefronts, pony rides, a petting zoo, a shooting gallery, gold panning, a Mystery Mine, a carriage collection and that old standby of Old West theme parks, hourly gunfights in the street. ~ 100 Ponderosa Road, Incline Village; 775-831-0691, ATV reservations 775-832-7433; www.ponderosaranch.com.

Across the road, the nine-story-tall **Cal-Neva Resort** out on the end of Stateline Point was owned by Frank Sinatra in the 1960s. Celebrities of that era, including Bob Hope, Bing Crosby and Sinatra's "Rat Pack," made it their vacation haunt. Marilyn Monroe spent so much time there that a personal chalet was built for her on the grounds. ~ 2 Stateline Road, Crystal Bay; 775-832-4000, 800-225-6382; www.calnevaresort.com, e-mail resmgr@calnevaresort.com.

Route 28 skirts the bay to **Incline Village** on the far side. The village was originally the center for the logging industry that shipped millions of board feet of timber from Lake Tahoe across the Washoe Valley to the mining town of Virginia City, Nevada, the region's largest community during the Comstock Lode silver boom, which started 1859. Now made up mostly of large vacation homes, Incline Village is an alpine skiing and golf center, as well as the location of **Ponderosa Ranch**, Lake Tahoe's only major theme park.

At Incline Village, Route 431 turns off the lake shore road and makes its steep, winding way up the sides of massive **Mount Rose** and **Slide Mountain**, the one with the broadcast towers on top that's visible from almost any point on the lake. On the other side of the mountain, Route 431 plunges down into the Washoe Valley to come out a few miles south of Reno. If you're not going that way, it's still worth the short detour to drive up to the spectacular vista point a few miles above Incline Village.

A few miles south along the ponderosa-studded shoreline lies **Sand Harbor**, the northern unit of **Lake Tahoe–Nevada State Park**. The park is set on a point of land with a sandy beach on one side and a rocky shore on the other. It's ideally situated for swimming and has paved walking trails, picnic areas, restrooms and a boat launch, as well as a permanent outdoor theater stage for the Shakespeare festival held here in August. Day-use fee, $6 per vehicle. ~ 775-831-0494; www.state.nv.us/stparks.

Beach at Sand Harbor.

The 14,000-acre Lake Tahoe–Nevada State Park is the largest state park in the Lake Tahoe Basin, but for much of the drive down the East Shore you'll see no indication that you're within its boundaries. A couple of miles past Sand Harbor, the road veers away from the lake as the steep ridge of Deadman Point begins its 700-foot rise, hiding the lake from view. At the intersection of Routes 28 and 50, Lake Tahoe–Nevada State Park's **Spooner Lake** has a picnic area and an easy nature trail around the shore of a pretty, wooded lake. Day-use fee, $5 per vehicle. ~ Route 50; 775-831-0494; www.state.nv.us/stparks.

Here Route 28 ends, but the East Shore drive continues as it merges with Route 50 from Carson City, just ten miles away. When you finally return to the lakeshore at the community of Glenbrook, driving high above the waterline, look toward the south to the highrise casino resorts of Stateline, still several miles ahead. Soon you reach the **Cave Rock** unit of Lake Tahoe–Nevada State Park, a popular shore-fishing spot with a picnic area, a small beach and a boat launch ramp. Cave Rock itself is the big volcanic formation where the road goes through a tunnel. Day-use fee, $5 per vehicle. ~ 775-831-0494; www.state.nv.us/stparks.

Leaving the state park, the road begins to pass residential communities that increase in size as you proceed farther south. Past **Zephyr Cove**, the East Shore's largest marina, you'll go around the back side of 500-foot-high Round Mound. If you take a right on the road that turns off just past the mound and drive around it to the lake side, you'll find yourself on **Nevada Beach**, possibly the most inviting strand of beach in the South Lake Tahoe/Stateline area, with its sand dunes, picnic area and restrooms. Parking fee. ~ Elk Point Road, Stateline; 775-589-4908.

Cave Rock.

Then suddenly you're back in the "city." With its cluster of tall, modern casino resorts, **Stateline** is Lake Tahoe's answer to the Las Vegas Strip. Of course, there's no volcano, roller coaster or Eiffel tower, but in these parts, where few structures stand more than two stories tall, the towering casino resorts are impressive enough without the gimmicks. The last in line, Harvey's Casino & Resort, stands just inches from the California state line and Heavenly Lake Tahoe ski resort, where our tour around Lake Tahoe started three chapters ago.

outdoor adventures

HIKING

The best day-hiking (distances for all hiking trails are one-way unless otherwise noted) on the Nevada side of Lake Tahoe starts from the vicinity of the mountain pass on Route 451 near the summit of Mount Rose. From the parking area just past Incline Lake, the **Tahoe Meadows Trail** is part of the Tahoe Rim Trail. This is the most painless way to try the rim trail because it's the highest trailhead, eliminating

An Outlet of Activity

The largest marina on Lake Tahoe's East Shore, Zephyr Cove offers a number of recreational pursuits. **Zephyr Cove Marina** rents boats of all kinds, from pedalboats, kayaks and one-, two- or three-passenger Waverunners to ski boats and 24-foot deck boats. Deep-lake sportfishing charters can be arranged as well. ~ 760 Route 50, Zephyr Cove; 755-589-4908; www.zephyrcove.com. The marina is also the base of operations for the ***Woodwind II***, a 55-foot glass-bottomed sailing catamaran that takes passengers on trips to Cave Rock and out into the middle of the lake. ~ Zephyr Cove; 775-588-3000.

Landlubbers are well cared for by **Zephyr Cove Resort Stables**, which leads guided one-to two-hour tours, including breakfast, lunch or dinner rides. Rides follow national forest trails through ponderosa forest with views of Lake Tahoe below. Reservations are recommended. ~ Zephyr Cove; 775-588-5664; zephyrcove stables.com.

most of the climb to the upper ridges. There is a 1.3-mile paved loop for a short, easy hike across alpine meadows that spring to vibrant life with wildflowers in early summer. If you wish, you can continue south as far as you want from where the pavement ends. The next Tahoe Rim trailhead is at Spooner Summit, 21 miles south on Route 50.

For a more challenging hike in the same area, climb to the **Mount Rose Summit**, a 6-mile hike with a 2000-foot elevation gain to the mountaintop at 10,776 feet above sea level. The trail starts as a gated dirt road from a parking pullout about a half-mile below the pass. Leaving the road, the trail eases down across a lush meadow and then climbs to a saddle on the west side of the mountain. Switchbacking up fields of volcanic rock and gravel, it finally reaches the summit for a 360-degree view of Lake Tahoe, the Mount Rose Wilderness and the Washoe Valley.

Farther south along the shore, the moderate 1.5-mile **Slaughterhouse Canyon Trail** starts at a primitive road with

Flying down the Flume

The **Flume Trail** (4.4 miles each way from Marlette Lake; 10.4 miles from Spooner Lake) is one of the most famous mountain bike rides in the Sierra Nevada. It starts with a long uphill grind through the aspens from Spooner Lake to Marlette Lake (see "Hiking" above). Past the cutoff to the Tahoe Rim Trail, you coast down to the dam on Marlette Lake, where you pick up the Flume Trail itself. It's a rediscovered portion of an old logging flume that was used to float timber down to a pickup point for a sawmill back in the 1860s. The trail itself is dead straight and not very steep at all, but it is quite narrow and traverses a near-vertical slope 1600 feet above Lake Tahoe–spectacular . . . and scary! It ends at sandy Tunnel Creek Road, which descends sharply to Ponderosa Ranch. Careful–more bike accidents happen on this road than on the Flume Trail itself. Return to Spooner Lake on Route 28.

Mountain bike rentals are available at **Village Bicycles** (800 Tahoe Boulevard, Incline Village; 775-831-3537), **Shoreline Bike Shop** (259 Kingsbury Grade, Stateline; 775-588-8777) and **Spooner Lake Outdoor Company** (Spooner Lake; 775-749-5349, 888-858-8844; www.flumetrail.com). Spooner also offers guided mountain bike trips limited to six riders.

a locked gate on the west side of Route 28 about 4.5 miles south of Sand Harbor in Lake Tahoe–Nevada State Park. This is actually two hikes in one; after the first half-mile, the road divides. Turn right and you're on your way to the beach at Skunk Harbor, probably the most secluded beach on the entire lake. A left turn takes you to **Prey Meadows**, an idyllic spot filled with flowers in the spring. For a longer hike, you can continue another 3.5 miles downstream from the meadows through V-shaped Slaughterhouse Canyon. The trail eventually comes out on the Glenbrook Golf Course.

For an all-day, 11-mile loop trip that takes in a segment of the Tahoe Rim Trail, tackle the hike to **Marlette Lake**. Leave your car in the parking lot (fee) at Spooner Lake, just off Route 50 at the junction with Route 28. Hike five miles up the four-wheel-drive road to Marlette Lake, a route you can expect to share with mountain bikers and horseback riders. The road takes you gently uphill through groves of aspen, then makes a sharp ascent to a ridge overlooking beautiful Marlette Lake. There's no fishing in this lake, which is used as a natural fish hatchery by the Nevada Division of Wildlife. Less than half a mile south of the lake, a side trail to the right climbs by switchbacks partway up the west face of 9214-foot Snow Valley Peak to intercept the Tahoe Rim Trail, which descends a long ridgeline into the forest, eventually returning to Route 50 at Spooner Summit, about one mile uphill from the parking area at Spooner Lake where you started.

GOLF

The **Golf Courses at Incline Village** are two 18-hole courses, both designed by Robert Trent Jones, Jr.—a 6915-yard, par-72 championship course with bunkered greens and lateral water hazards on almost every hole, and a 6515-yard, par-58 mountain course laid out in switchback formation around the natural challenges of creeks, pine forest and rock formations, with views of Lake Tahoe. Club and cart rentals are available. Open May through October. ~ Championship Course: 955 Fairway Boulevard, Incline Village; Mountain Course: 690 Wilson Way, Incline Village; both courses 702-832-1144; www.golfincline.com.

At Stateline, right at the water's edge, **Edgewood Tahoe Golf Course** is generally considered to be the finest course in the Lake Tahoe area, if not the entire Sierra Nevada. Rated one of America's 100 Greatest Golf Courses by *Golf Digest,* it has the highest green fees and the hardest-to-get tee times around. Designed in 1969 by George Fazio, the generally level 18-hole, par-72, course is 7491 yards in length with fairways bounded by more water than trees. Cart and club rentals are available. Open May through October. ~ 180 Lake Parkway, Stateline; 775-588-8049; www.edgewood-tahoe.com.

FISHING

Both the Sand Harbor and Cave Rock units of **Lake Tahoe–Nevada State Park** are considered to be among the best spots on the lake for shore fishing.

Lake Tahoe–Nevada State Park's **Spooner Lake** is a year-round favorite for flyfishing, catch-and-release only, regularly seeded with cutthroat trout and sometimes rainbow and brown trout. Kokanee salmon is a prized species. Ice-fishing is allowed in winter. ~ Route 50; 775-831-0494; www.state.nv.us/stparks.

SKIING

The highest ski area base in the Lake Tahoe area is at **Mount Rose**, sprawling across 900 skiable acres with 41 runs up to 2.5 miles long, with a vertical drop of 1440 feet from the 9700-foot summit. There are five quad and triple chairlifts. The lake views from the slopes are incomparable.

Runs, including both trails and a large bowl, are rated 30 percent beginner, 35 percent intermediate and 35 percent expert. Snowboarding is allowed, and standard and high-performance ski packages as well as snowboards are for rent. ~ 2222 Route 431; 775-849-0704, 800-754-7673; www.skirose.com, e-mail deepsnow@skirose.com.

Diamond Peak Ski Area at Incline Village is an affordable, moderate-sized ski resort with 30 runs spanning 655 skiable acres of open glades and forest trails. The longest of six chairlifts runs to the summit of 8540-foot Diamond Peak, providing access to expert trails at Crystal Ridge, the Great Flume and Solitude Canyon. The longest run is 2.5 miles, with a vertical drop of 1840 feet. Runs are rated 18 percent beginner, 46 percent intermediate and 36 percent advanced. There's also a snowboard terrain park and superpipe. Standard ski package and snowboard rentals are available. ~ 1210 Ski Way, Incline Village; 775-832-1177, snow conditions 775-831-3211; www.diamondpeak.com, e-mail info@diamondpeak.com.

For skinny-skiers, there are 90 kilometers of groomed trails at the **Spooner Lake Cross Country Ski Area**, including routes around the lake, across Spooner Meadow and up through the aspen glades of beautiful North Canyon. If you ski on two consecutive days, the second day's trail pass is half-price. Cross-country ski rentals and snowshoe rentals are available, and there's shuttle service from South Lake Tahoe and Incline Village. ~ Route 50 at Route 28; 775-749-5349, snow conditions 775-887-8844; www.spoonerlake.com, e-mail spoonerlake@pyramid.net.

INDOOR ADVENTURES

The **Incline Village Recreation Center** is a good place to get your body moving when the weather outside is lousy. It has a 25-yard, eight-lane heated swimming pool, a basketball court and a workout room with strength training machines. There are classes in aerobics, ballet, jazz dance, stretch, yoga and cardio-kickboxing. Drop-ins are welcome for a daily fee. ~ 980 Incline Way, Incline Village; 775-832-1300.

Another place to find indoor action, **Bowl Incline** not only has bowling alleys but also pool tables, a full-swing golf simulator, a video arcade and video poker machines. ~ 920 Southwood, Incline Village; 775-831-1900.

CAMPING

Privately operated under a national forest special-use permit, **Zephyr Cove Campground** has 150 wooded tent/RV sites at a distance from the shoreline with a dumping station and full hookups that can accommodate motorhomes up to 40 feet. Located at the edge of a small, pretty sand beach, the campground has restrooms and showers, and each site has a picnic table and barbecue grill. Sites cost $48 per night. Open April through October. ~ 775-589-4981.

The forest service's **Nevada Beach Campground** is set at the edge of a long, straight, sandy beach with a lit-up nighttime view of the Stateline skyline. It has 54 sites for tents/RVs (up to 45 feet long), with picnic tables and grills. There are restrooms, showers and a dumping station but no hookups. Sites cost $22 to $24 per night. Open May to mid-October. ~ 775-588-5562; reservations 877-444-6777; www.reserveusa.com.

lodging

In Crystal Bay, the **Tahoe Biltmore** seems much bigger on the inside than it does on the outside. Guest rooms in both the main hotel and the adjoining motor lodge sport simple, contemporary decor with earth tones and light-colored wood. Although the views can't rival those from the Cal-Neva across the road, the old stone-and-woodbeam hotel with its shady past is steeped in neo-Gothic atmosphere that makes it seem romantic and mysterious on wintery or foggy nights. ~ 5 Route 28, Crystal Bay; 775-831-0660, 800-245-8667; www.tahoebiltmore.com, e-mail fun@tahoebiltmore.com. MODERATE.

The **Cal-Neva Resort** has 220 rooms with traditional period reproduction furnishings. The hotel is situated on a point

extending out into the lake, so all rooms have views of the water through windows framed by elaborate draperies. Suites have walkout balconies and fireplaces. For a substantially higher rate, you can rent the special chalet once reserved for Marilyn Monroe. ~ 2 Stateline Road, Crystal Bay; 775-832-4000, 800-225-6382; www.calnevaresort.com, e-mail resmgr@calnevaresort.com. MODERATE TO DELUXE.

In Stateline, the 19-story **Harvey's Casino & Resort** is the largest hotel in the Lake Tahoe area, with 740 rooms and suites in a wide range of sizes, most with lake or mountain views. In- room amenities include such small luxuries as hair dryers, honor bars and video games. ~ Casino Center, Stateline; 775-588-2411, 800-745-4320; www.harveys-tahoe.com. DELUXE TO ULTRA-DELUXE.

Harrah's Lake Tahoe stands 18 stories tall and has 532 exceptionally spacious rooms, decorated in contemporary style without the garish color schemes or chrome-plated wallpaper that so many casino hotels use to drive you out of the room and down to the gaming tables. Then again, the TVs have pay-to-play in-room video games, so machines have a chance to get your money one way or another. There's an indoor heated swimming pool. ~ Casino Center, Stateline; 775-588-6611, 800-

427-7247, fax 775-586-6607; www.harrahstahoe.com. DELUXE TO ULTRA-DELUXE.

In the 1970s, when Elvis and Sinatra graced its stage and penthouse suite, Las Vegas' Caesars Palace was the ultimate luxury hotel on the Strip. Today, dwarfed by the towering replicas of international cities that surround it, Caesars in Vegas is almost quaint, but its new location, **Caesars Tahoe**, preserves a little of that old fantasyland ostentation. Most of the 440 guest rooms feature Roman styling, with column and faux marble trim, and have jacuzzis or two-person tubs. Suites come in five showy styles: Roman, Hollywood, Asian, Caribbean and futuristic. There are a heated indoor pool, a sauna, a spa and lighted tennis courts. ~ Casino Center, Stateline; 775-588-3515, 800-648-3353, fax 775-586-2068; www.caesars.com. MODERATE TO ULTRA-DELUXE.

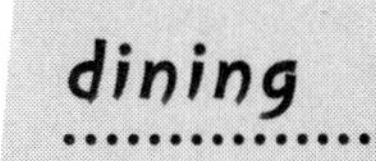

The **Café Biltmore** offers some of the best meal bargains on the North Shore–like three-egg *huevos rancheros* and huge salads any time of the day or evening and prime rib and salmon combination dinners from 4 p.m. on. A pretty garden outside the windows helps the rather plain decor. Beware of the one-armed bandits on the way out. ~ Tahoe Biltmore, 5 Route 28, Crystal Bay; 775-831-0660, 800-245-8667; www.tahoebiltmore.com, e-mail fun@tahoebiltmore.com.

At the other end of the lake and the price spectrum, **Llewellyns** is among the highest-priced restaurants on the South Shore and worth it. The waitstaff is dignified and dressed to the hilt, and the lake view from the 19th floor of Harvey's Casino & Resort is superb. Try the Thai curry frog legs, lobster bisque, venison medallions or vegetarian combination plate. The

FILL 'ER UP

Best of the casino buffets in Stateline is the **Roman Feast** at Caesars Tahoe. Featured items in this attractively presented all-you-can-eat binge include rotisserie prime rib, pizza, pasta and Asian stir-fry. There's a Friday seafood buffet, a Saturday steak buffet and a Sunday champagne brunch. The ambience is that of a cafeteria with Roman columns. ~ Casino Center, Stateline; 775-588-3515; www.caesars.com. MODERATE.

time to dine here, if you can get reservations, is when the curtains over the windows are opened with much pomp and ceremony to unveil a magnificent sunset panorama. ~ Casino Center, Stateline; 775-588-2411; www.harveys-tahoe.com. DELUXE TO ULTRA-DELUXE.

The other full-service restaurant in the same hotel, the **Sage Room** opened in 1947 along with the original card room that grew into Harvey's Casino & Resort. It started as a steakhouse, and the staple is still the sizzling meat, though the menu has evolved to encompass lobster and other selections like rabbit sausage pasta. Dim, hushed, candlelit and unbelievably romantic, it continues to set the standard for fine dining at Lake Tahoe. ~ Casino Center, Stateline; 775-588-2411; www.harveys-tahoe.com. ULTRA-DELUXE.

The formal **Summit Room** is Harrah's Lake Tahoe's unabashed attempt to compete with the Sage Room. It succeeds pretty well, too, especially if you like to dress for dinner. On the hotel's 16th and 17th floors, it occupies spaces that were originally suites reserved for celebrities, and with only 25 tables it's so intimate it almost feels like Wayne Newton is sharing your table. The menu changes weekly. ~ Casino Center, Stateline; 775-588-6611; www.harrahstahoe.com. ULTRA-DELUXE.

nightlife

On the North Shore, the **Tahoe Biltmore** presents an array of musicians. ~ 5 Route 28, Crystal Bay; 775-831-0660, 800-245-8667.

Stateline's only full—scale Las Vegas—style showroom is the **Circus Maximus** in Caesars Tahoe, where acts such as Daryl Hall & John Oates and Big Head Todd and the Monsters sometimes perform. ~ Casino Center, Stateline; 775-586-2044, 800-648-3535. The **South Shore Room** in

Harrah's Tahoe also features name musicians. ~ Casino Center, Stateline; 775-588-6611, 800-427-7247.

In Horizon Casino Resort's **Golden Cabaret**, female impersonators pose as celebrities, while the old showroom where Elvis Presley used to play has been replaced by a multiplex movie theater. ~ Casino Center, Stateline; 775-588-6211, 800-683-8266.

index

lodging & dining index

HIDDEN GUIDES

Adventure travel or a relaxing vacation?—"Hidden" guidebooks are the only travel books in the business to provide detailed information on both. Aimed at environmentally aware travelers, our motto is "Where Vacations Meet Adventures." These books combine details on unique hotels, restaurants and sightseeing with information on camping, sports and hiking for the outdoor enthusiast.

THE NEW KEY GUIDES

Based on the concept of ecotourism, The New Key Guides are dedicated to the preservation of Central America's rare and endangered species, architecture and archaeology. Filled with helpful tips, they give travelers everything they need to know about these exotic destinations.

Ulysses Press books are available at bookstores everywhere. If any of the following titles are unavailable at your local bookstore, ask the bookseller to order them.

You can also order books directly from Ulysses Press
P.O. Box 3440, Berkeley, CA 94703
800-377-2542 or 510-601-8301
fax: 510-601-8307
www.ulyssespress.com
e-mail: ulysses@ulyssespress.com

about the author

Richard Harris has written or co-written 31 other guidebooks including Ulysses' *Weekend Adventure Getaways: Monterey, Carmel, Big Sur, Santa Cruz*; *Hidden Baja*; *Hidden Cancún and the Yucatán* and the bestselling *Hidden Southwest.* He has also served as contributing editor on guides to Mexico, New Mexico, and other ports of call for John Muir Publications, Fodor's, Birnbaum and Access guides. He is a past president of PEN New Mexico and currently president of the New Mexico Book Association. When not traveling, Richard writes and lives in Santa Fe, New Mexico.

about the photographer

Lee Foster is a travel photographer/writer based in Berkeley, California. Lee's website (www.fostertravel.com) presents over 200 worldwide destinations, including his speciality, Northern California. His most recent book is *Northern California History Weekends* (Globe Pequot). Lee provides travel photos and writing for major print publications, from *Travel & Leisure* to the *New York Times.* He has won seven Lowell Thomas Awards, the highest awards in travel journalism, and has been named Lowell Thomas Travel Journalist of the Year, Silver Winner.